Woodworking

Techniques & Projects for the First-Time Woodworker

John Kelsey

FOX CHAPEL
PUBLISHING

© 2008, 2013 by John Kelsey and Fox Chapel Publishing Company, Inc., East Petersburg, PA.

Woodworking, Revised and Expanded (2013) is a revised edition of *Woodworking* (2008), published by Fox Chapel Publishing Company, Inc. Revisions include new projects. The projects Butterfly House and Coffee Can Birdhouse are adapted from the book *Easy-to-Build Outdoor & Deck Projects* (2005), published by Fox Chapel Publishing. The patterns contained herein are copyrighted by the authors. Readers may make copies of these patterns for personal use. The patterns themselves, however, are not to be duplicated for resale or distribution under any circumstances. Any such copying is a violation of copyright law.

ISBN 978-1-56523-801-5

Library of Congress Cataloging-in-Publication Data

Kelsey, John, 1946-
  Woodworking / John Kelsey. -- Revised and expanded.
      pages cm. -- (DIY crafts)
  ISBN 978-1-56523-801-5
  1. Woodwork. 2. Woodwork--Handbooks, manuals, etc. 3. Carpentry. 4. Carpentry--Handbooks, manuals, etc. I. Title.
  TT185.K375 2013
  684'.08--dc23
                            2013017981

To learn more about the other great books from Fox Chapel Publishing, or to find a retailer near you, call toll-free
800-457-9112 or visit us at *www.FoxChapelPublishing.com*.

Note to Authors: We are always looking for talented authors to write new books. Please send a brief letter
describing your idea to Acquisition Editor, 1970 Broad Street, East Petersburg, PA 17520.

Printed in China
First printing

Table of Contents

How to Use This Book

Welcome to woodworking!

In this book, you will find 23 fun woodworking projects designed to help you learn basic woodworking skills. You can build these projects in any order you like. However, if you would like to learn all of the skills and techniques you might need, please start at the beginning and proceed step-by-step.

In this way you will learn seven fundamental woodworking skills.

You will learn how to:

1. read drawings, measure, and transfer dimensions,
2. choose suitable wood for your project,
3. saw square edges and ends in wood,
4. drill round holes and saw other curved shapes,
5. join wood using nails and glue,
6. sand wood to create smooth surfaces, edges, and corners, and
7. finish off your project with paint or varnish.

Once you are familiar with the basic tools, materials, and safety procedures, you'll be ready to tackle almost any project.

Note

This book of woodworking projects and techniques has been designed to entice, instruct, and entertain beginner woodcarvers, including children as young as 9. The projects offer a sequential set of basic woodworking skills beginners can learn that allow them to build a variety of woodworking items, including toys, gifts, and furniture they can actually use.

Every project uses the same kit of simple hand tools. The discussion on supplies and tools (Chapters 2 and 3) includes step-by-step demonstrations with practice exercises. These skills are used throughout the book.

Acquiring woodworking skills will enrich your life, increase self-confidence, and help you develop a savvy, can-do attitude toward problem solving.

If you are an adult using this book to teach a child, please read the following. Parents can work together with their children, but group leaders and teachers should complete each project before introducing it to kids. If a group works on the project, kids can double and triple up on sets of tools. Leaders with a large group and a shortage of equipment might consider setting up workstations for each operation and cycling the kids through the stations.

Finally, remember that the best approach in teaching children is to first demonstrate a task and then supervise as they attempt it themselves. Let them try new things and make their own mistakes; they can always cut another piece of wood. Keep woodworking a fun and enjoyable experience.

Chapter 1

All About Wood

Did you know the following wood facts?

- There are many different kinds or species of wood, because there are many different species of trees. They have names you've probably heard, such as oak, pine, and maple. Different wood species are different colors, and some species are harder and stronger than others.
- Wood, unlike metal and plastic, is not the same all the way through. It's built in layers we call annual rings, because the living tree adds a new annual ring every year.
- When you look at a tree stump, or the end of a piece of firewood, you'll see the circular pattern of annual rings. The ring at the log's center, called pith, is wood formed during the tree's first year of life.
- Every branch begins at the pith and grows outward from it. Knots in a board are the stubs of tree branches.
- The annual rings create beautiful patterns on the surface of a piece of wood. They're called the wood figure.
- Wood is made of long, thin fibers growing in the same direction up and down the tree trunk. They're called the wood grain.
- A piece of wood doesn't stay the same size. It gets bigger and smaller along with the amount of water vapor in the air.
- When we saw a tree trunk into boards, we slice it lengthwise like a submarine sandwich, not crosswise like a salami. Sometimes we start sawing at one edge of the tree trunk, with every slice right next to the one before. This is called plainsawing. Other times we make every cut go through the center of the tree. This is called quartersawing. The way we saw the tree determines how boards look, and behave.

How Old Is That Tree?

Can you tell how old a tree is? It's easy! Remember that a new annual ring is formed each year a tree is alive. After a tree is cut down, you can count the rings on the stump to figure out the tree's age. The rings can also give us clues about the tree's history. A wide ring usually means a good year, while a narrow ring suggests a bad one.

You don't have to kill a tree to learn its secrets. Foresters now use a tool called an increment borer to pull out a pencil-sized plug of wood from the tree trunk. Then, they count the rings on the plug to determine the age of the tree.

Many kinds of trees can live to be 200 years or more. The oldest living trees are the gnarly bristlecone pine trees that grow high in the Rocky Mountains in California. They can live to be a whopping 5,000 years old. Imagine counting those rings!

Even though they aren't the oldest, the giant redwoods in California are the world's largest trees. Some are more than 1,000 years old. The biggest redwood (and the biggest tree in the world) is the General Sherman Tree in Sequoia National Park, California.

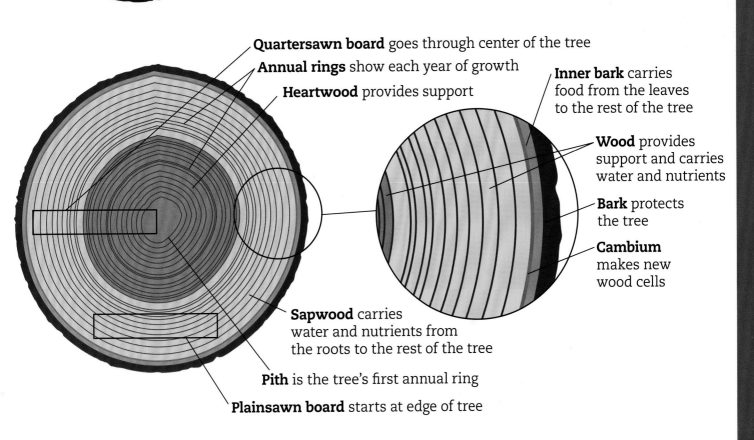

Quartersawn board goes through center of the tree

Annual rings show each year of growth

Heartwood provides support

Inner bark carries food from the leaves to the rest of the tree

Wood provides support and carries water and nutrients

Bark protects the tree

Cambium makes new wood cells

Sapwood carries water and nutrients from the roots to the rest of the tree

Pith is the tree's first annual ring

Plainsawn board starts at edge of tree

How to Select Wood

Just as you have traits that help people recognize who you are, like brown eyes or red hair, wood has certain traits or characteristics too. Learning about all of these different traits can help you decide what wood is best for your projects.

Wood Figure

Remember that we just learned how wood is made up of annual rings and microscopic fibers? Well, those rings and fibers create the lines and swirls that you see on the face, or surface, of a board. What we see on the surface is commonly called wood grain or figure.

Most people find wood figure attractive and look for special figure in the pieces they buy. Stain and varnish are brushed on wood to bring out the wood figure even more. When you select boards, check for figure that will enhance the beauty and design of your woodworking projects.

How the annual rings appear on a board also tells us where it grew inside the tree, what the figure will be like, and how it was cut. If you see the curve of the annual rings on the end of a board, the board is plainsawn and will show arches and whorls on the face. If the rings run up and down on the end of the board, the board was quartersawn, and the figure will be mostly straight lines. Plainsawn wood is more likely to cup than quartersawn wood. Knowing the difference between these types of cuts can help you check for defects and choose the easiest type of wood to use. Understanding the direction the grain runs also helps you determine the best way to cut.

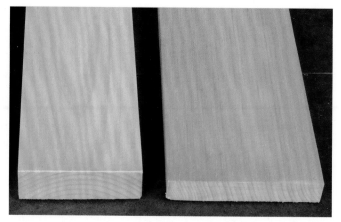

The left board is plainsawn and has arches, while the right board shows the straight figure of quartersawing.

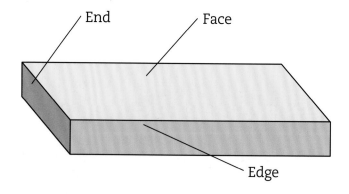

Wood is easy to split parallel to its fibers, or with the grain.

Wood is difficult to split perpendicular to the fibers, or across the grain.

Wood Defects

Whenever you select wood, inspect the boards carefully. Choose straight, flat boards with small knots or no knots at all. Do not choose boards with large cracks and splits or sticky pitch pockets. Watch out for boards cut from the center of the tree, too. Remember, that is the pith, and boards cut from it will probably cup, or curve across the width. Here is list of wood defects you should try to avoid.

Cup: Wood that curves across the width of the board is cupped. This kind of wood is okay to use for most projects.

Knots: The stubs of branches that the tree has grown around are called knots. Stay away from these because you can't drive a nail into a knot.

Pitch Pockets: Sticky globs of sap that ooze from the wood are called pitch pockets. Sap is messy and cannot be easily washed off.

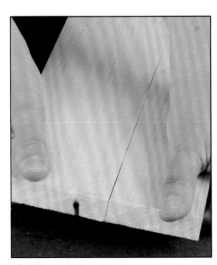

Splits or Checks: Long cracks that can't be pushed back together or glued are called splits or checks. You don't want any of these because they weaken the wood.

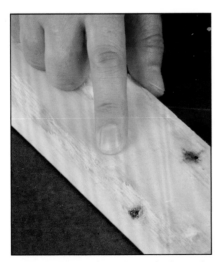

Wane: When the edge of a board has bark, it creates an irregular surface, called wane. Waney edges cannot be rebuilt, so try not to use these boards.

Warp: Wood that is wavy looking is said to be warped. You can see this by viewing the board from the end. If you're working on small projects, you can sometimes cut around the warp, but straight boards work best.

Hardwood and Softwood

If you've ever chewed on a pencil or hit a ball with a baseball bat, you've probably noticed some woods are softer than others. In fact, they are usually divided into two broad categories: hardwoods and softwoods. Often, softwoods are softer than hardwoods, but that isn't always true.

Hardwood comes from deciduous trees, which lose their leaves in the fall. Oak and maple, for example, are hardwoods. These woods are mostly used to make strong furniture, flooring, wall paneling, and tools.

Coniferous trees, also called softwoods, keep their needles all year.

Deciduous trees, or hardwoods, lose their leaves in the fall.

Softwood is from coniferous trees, which keep their needles year round. Pine and fir are types of softwood. These woods are used a lot in construction for building structures like houses and schools. They can also be used for smaller items like toy trains, planes, rocking horses, and other kinds of toys. Often, softwoods are easier to work with than hardwoods. This is something you should consider when choosing the wood for your projects.

Did you know both hardwoods and softwoods come in many different colors? Softwoods, like pine, fir, and spruce, are white, pale yellow, or pink, but cedar and redwood are dark red or reddish brown. Red oak, cherry, and walnut—all hardwoods—are red and brown, while maple, ash, and white oak are white.

Common Woods for Woodworking

This chart shows the basic characteristics of the most common softwoods and hardwoods and tells how each type might be used.

Hardwoods			
Wood	Color	Hardness, Workability	Uses
Ash	white	medium hard, coarse grain	tool handles, wood furniture
Cherry	rich orange-brown	medium hard, easy to work	furniture, cabinets
Maple	white	very hard, difficult to work, cuts cleanly	furniture, tools
Mahogany	brown	medium hard, easy to work	furniture, interiors
Red Oak	reddish tan	hard, difficult to work	furniture, flooring
Poplar	white, green-brown	soft, easy to work, easy to paint	furniture
Black Walnut	dark purple-brown	medium hard, easy to work	furniture, interiors

Softwoods			
Wood	Color	Hardness, Workability	Uses
White Pine	white, yellowy tan	soft, easy to work	furniture, moldings, plywood, toys
Red Cedar	brown	soft, easy to work	wall siding, paneling
Douglas Fir	pinky tan	medium hard, coarse grain	house construction, plywood
Spruce	white	soft, easy to work	house construction, musical instruments
California Redwood	brown	soft, easy to work	wall siding, paneling
Hemlock	brown	soft, easy to work	house construction
Aromatic Cedar	reddish brown	soft, easy to work	furniture, closet linings

Sources of Wood

Softwood and some hardwood lumbers are available at any home center or retail lumberyard. Hobby shops also sell some types of wood, but they can be expensive.

Small projects like the ones in this book do not use much wood. If someone in your family or your neighborhood is a builder or a woodworker, ask them whether they have short ends or scraps that you may have, like the stack in the photo.

Participate in spring clean-up in your home or school, and look for wooden discards you can use in a project. Even an old broom handle might be just what you need for handles or wheels!

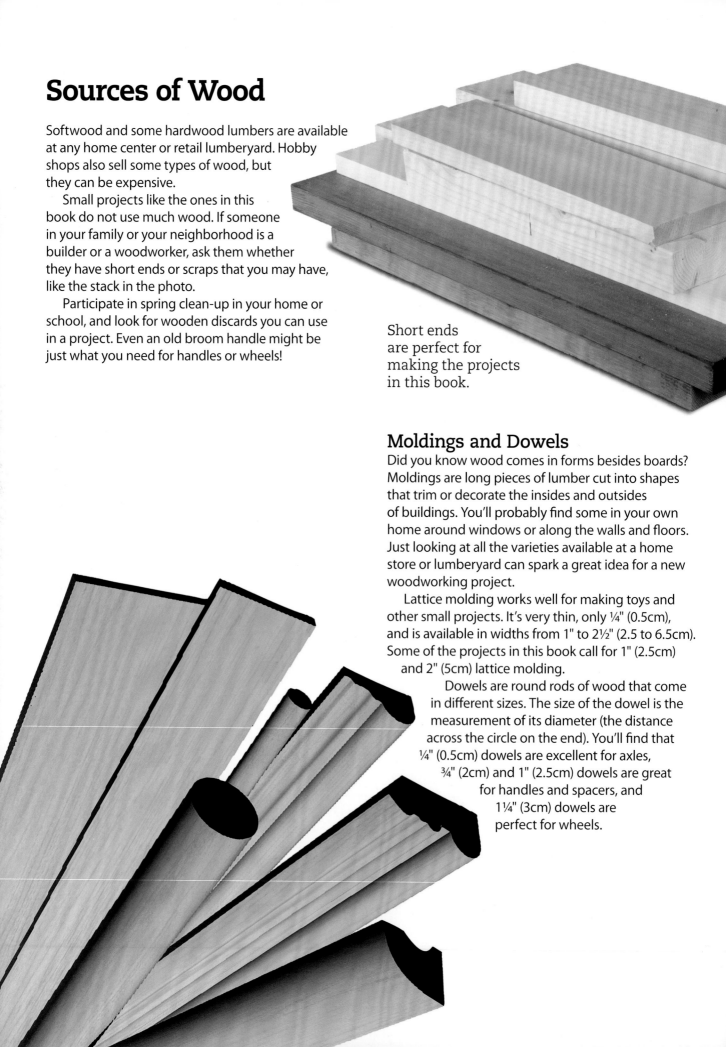

Short ends are perfect for making the projects in this book.

Moldings and Dowels

Did you know wood comes in forms besides boards? Moldings are long pieces of lumber cut into shapes that trim or decorate the insides and outsides of buildings. You'll probably find some in your own home around windows or along the walls and floors. Just looking at all the varieties available at a home store or lumberyard can spark a great idea for a new woodworking project.

Lattice molding works well for making toys and other small projects. It's very thin, only ¼" (0.5cm), and is available in widths from 1" to 2½" (2.5 to 6.5cm). Some of the projects in this book call for 1" (2.5cm) and 2" (5cm) lattice molding.

Dowels are round rods of wood that come in different sizes. The size of the dowel is the measurement of its diameter (the distance across the circle on the end). You'll find that ¼" (0.5cm) dowels are excellent for axles, ¾" (2cm) and 1" (2.5cm) dowels are great for handles and spacers, and 1¼" (3cm) dowels are perfect for wheels.

Wood Dimensions

Measuring lumber gets kind of tricky, so here's what you have to know. When you go to a lumberyard and ask for a pine board 6" (15cm) wide and 1" (2.5cm) thick, you'll actually get a board that measures 5½" (14cm) wide and ¾" (2cm) thick. That's because you pay for the size of the board before it was dried and planed (shaved smooth). Softwood boards are always ½" (1.5cm) or ¾" (2cm) narrower and ¼" (0.5cm) thinner than labeled. On the plus side, they are often a few inches longer.

Now, here's the tricky part. Even though you know it's not, that 5½" by ¾" (14 x 2cm) thick pine board is still labeled 1x6, and it is called a "one-by-six." All "one-by" softwood boards are called dimension lumber, and the size is the same everywhere. The projects in this book are scaled to use softwood boards at their actual width and thickness.

Because wood was once living, remember that its size will be affected by humidity (the water vapor in the air). When it is humid, wood expands. When it's dry, wood shrinks. It does not expand or shrink much, but it changes enough that woodworkers allow for this wood movement.

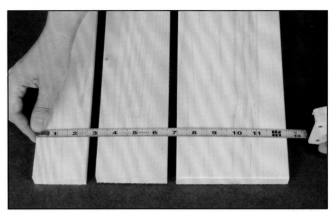

When you measure a 1x3 (left), you'll find it is only 1½" (4cm) wide. The 1x4 is 3½" (9cm) wide, and the 1x6 is 5½" (14cm) wide.

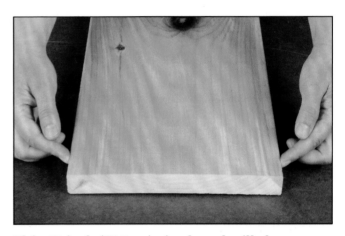

This 10-inch (25.5cm) pine board will change in width as the air becomes wetter or drier. It might change by as much as ¼" (0.5cm).

Actual Wood Dimensions		
Name	**Actual Thickness**	**Actual Width**
1x2	¾" (2cm)	1½" (4cm)
1x3	¾" (2cm)	2½" (6.5cm)
1x4	¾" (2cm)	3½" (9cm)
1x6	¾" (2cm)	5½" (14cm)
1x8	¾" (2cm)	7¼" (18.5cm)
1x10	¾" (2cm)	9¼" (23.5cm)
1x12	¾" (2cm)	11¼" (28.5cm)
2x2	1½" (4cm)	1½" (4cm)
2x4	1½" (4cm)	3½" (9cm)
2x6	1½" (4cm)	5½" (14cm)

Chapter 2

Woodworking Supplies

Along with wood, tools, and a good place to work, you will need the supplies in this chapter. You'll learn how to use all of them later in this book.

Sandpaper

Sandpaper is used to smooth wood before glue or finish is applied. It is made of abrasive particles that are glued onto a paper backing. Sandpaper comes in sheets the size of notebook paper and has different grits or grades—coarse, medium, fine, and very fine. Each grit has corresponding numbers printed on the back of a sheet. For example, 80-grit paper is coarse, 100-grit is medium, 150-grit is fine, and 220-grit is very fine. Most projects need medium, fine, and very fine sandpaper.

- **Garnet sandpaper** is orangey-brown, inexpensive, and best for hand sanding.
- **Aluminum oxide (AlOx) sandpaper** is gray or brown and about the same price as garnet.
- **Black silicon-carbide sandpaper** comes in extremely fine grits of 400 and 600. Use it to sand between coats of varnish and to sharpen chisels and knives.
- **Steel wool**, though not actually sandpaper, has similar uses. It can scrub projects, smooth varnish between coats, or remove dirt and rust from old tools. Be sure to wear gloves to protect your hands!

Sandpaper Grits

This chart shows the different types of sandpaper and their uses. The grit numbers stamped on the back of sandpaper tell you whether it is coarse or fine. For the projects in this book, choose the grits marked below with an asterisk.

Grit Number	Name	Purpose
60-grit	very coarse	removing old paint, shaping wood
80-grit	coarse	shaping wood, removing scratches, rounding edges
*100-grit	medium	shaping wood, removing scratches, rounding edges
120-grit	medium	removing scratches, smoothing surfaces
*150-grit	fine	smoothing surfaces, final sanding before finishing
180-grit	very fine	final sanding before finishing
*220-grit	very fine	sanding between coats of finish

Nails

There are many different kinds of nails, and they can be used to hold softwood lumber projects together. However, you have to choose the right nail for the job. It must be long enough to go all the way through the first piece of wood and most of the way into the second piece. For ¾" (2cm) thick wood, use 1½" (4cm).

Nails are identified by length, head type, and finish. The length is sometimes given in pennies, a very old measurement system. The symbol for pennies is the letter d, so a 16d nail is a sixteen-penny nail. The greater the number, the longer and thicker the nail. The chart below shows inch measurements for many d sizes.

If you don't want to see nail heads on your project, you can sometimes use a nail set (see Chapter 3, "Tools," page 33) to sink the heads below the wood's surface. To learn how to drive nails, see page 29.

Nail Sizes	
Nail size	**Length**
4d	1½" (4cm)
6d	2" (5cm)
8d	2½" (6.5cm)
10d	3" (7.5cm)
12d	3¼" (8.5cm)
16d	3½" (9cm)
20d	4" (10cm)

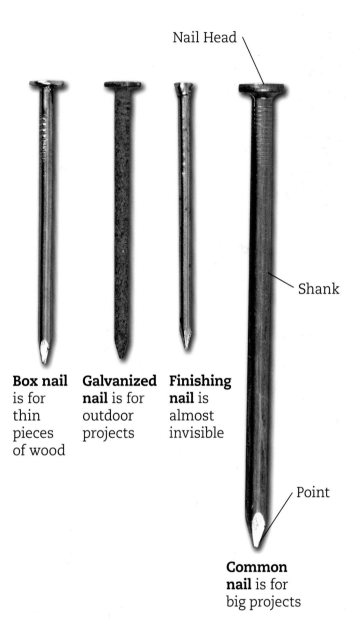

Nail Head

Shank

Point

Box nail is for thin pieces of wood

Galvanized nail is for outdoor projects

Finishing nail is almost invisible

Common nail is for big projects

Glue

Glue by itself can hold or join pieces of wood, but combining it with nails makes joined sections even stronger. Yellow wood glue is most often used for woodworking projects and can be bought at any home or hardware store. It's similar to the white glue you've probably used on craft projects, but it is stronger. If your project is likely to get wet, choose water-resistant yellow glue. At right are yellow wood glue, urethane glue, a glue stick, and epoxy glue. These other three glues may be useful in special cases, but yellow wood glue works best in most situations.

Yellow wood glue is an all-purpose woodworking glue

Urethane glue is a waterproof all-purpose glue

Glue stick temporarily glues patterns to wood

Epoxy glue holds wood to non-wood items

Skills:

Gluing Wood Together

Gluing requires more than just squeezing glue onto the wood surface. Before you do any gluing, brush all surfaces clean so that no sawdust sticks in the glue and weakens the bond.

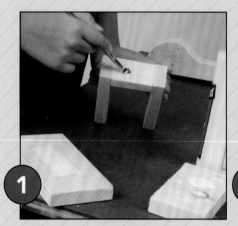

1

Spread the Glue. Make sure it is spread out evenly. Use a brush to apply the glue on both pieces of wood.

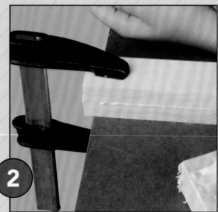

2

Clamp the Wood. Use clamps or a heavy weight on top. You have about 10 or 15 minutes before the glue dries. Extra glue will squeeze out of the joint and dribble down the wood. Wipe this off right away using a damp paper towel. Let the glue set overnight.

Epoxy glue

Epoxy has to be mixed from two tubes and used quickly before it sets. It is expensive, very strong, and waterproof. It's also messy and difficult to clean off your fingers. Choose epoxy if you want to glue metal to wood.

Urethane glue

Urethane glue is very strong, waterproof, and expensive. Like epoxy, it is messy and difficult to clean up, and almost impossible to clean off your fingers—it has to wear off. Urethane glue foams and expands as it sets, so it will fill gaps. Use it when you need its gap-filling ability.

Hot-melt glue

Hot-melt comes as a pen-sized cylinder of plastic. It has to be melted in a glue gun. Hot-melt glue sets very quickly but it is not very strong, and it comes out of the gun hot enough to cause a burn. It's best for tacking projects together temporarily, and for gluing fabric onto wood.

Super glue

Also called CA (cyanoacrylate) glue, and instant glue, super glue dries quickly and is extremely strong. It does not always bond well with wood, though it will glue your fingers together if you are not careful.

Glue Brush

Glue has to be evenly spread on both pieces of wood. To spread glue we use a stiff little brush, called a flux brush, which you can buy for a quarter at the hardware store. Use scissors to trim the brush to about half its length, either straight across or on an angle. Wash the brush after every gluing job, and it will last a long time. Don't wash it, and it will not be useable again.

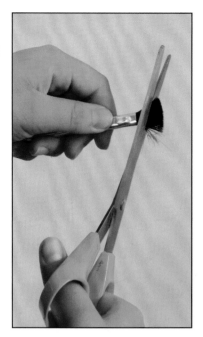

Be sure you clean the nozzle on the glue bottle, and put the cap back on, after each use. If it gets all clogged anyway, use an awl to pick the dried glue off.

Glue Goo

Yellow woodworking glue is not dangerous and won't glue your fingers together. The other glues—epoxy, super glue, urethane, and hot-melt—are nasty to get off your fingers, so wear disposable rubber gloves and spread newspaper on the work table.

Screws

Screws bite into the wood, so they get a much stronger grip than nails. Screws with glue make a really strong joint (see sidebar). Screws also do the best job holding hinges and other hardware. When you drive screws, start by drilling a little starter hole called a pilot hole. If you don't, the screw might not go straight, will be hard to drive, and might split the wood.

Screws are made with many different kinds of heads. Round-head screws have a dome-shaped head that sits on the surface of the project. Flat-head and bugle-head screws sit down flush with the surface. You must match the screwdriver to the screw head you want to use. Slotted-head or straight-slot screws are most common. Cross-head, also called Phillips head, are easiest to drive because they engage the screwdriver and keep it from slipping.

Screws are identified by their length, diameter, head, and driver, as well as by their finish. The diameter or gauge of a wood screw is usually given as a number (see chart). The higher the number, the thicker the screw. To learn how to drive screws, see page 40.

If you are using screws to join two pieces of wood, clamp them together while you drill the pilot hole. The chart at right shows what size pilot hole to drill.

Threads — Body — Head

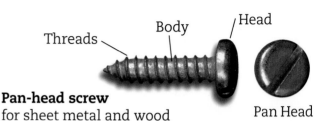

Pan-head screw
for sheet metal and wood

Pan Head

Machine screw
use with nuts and washers to make toys with moving joints

Round Head

Flat-head screw
head should be sunk below the wood's surface for joining two pieces of wood

Flat Head

Screw Gauge #	Shank size	Pilot hole
4	7⁄64" (2.8mm)	3⁄64" (1.2mm)
5	1⁄8" (3mm)	1⁄16" (2mm)
6	9⁄64" (3.6mm)	1⁄16" (2mm)
7	5⁄32" (4mm)	1⁄16" (2mm)
8	11⁄64" (4.4mm)	5⁄64" (1.9mm)
9	3⁄16" (5mm)	5⁄64" (1.9mm)
10	3⁄16" (5mm)	3⁄32" (2.5mm)

Hinges and Hardware

Because you will use some hardware for the projects in this book, it's important to understand exactly what hardware is and how to use it. Hinges, knobs, handles, and catches are all called hardware.

- **Hinges** let doors and lids swing open.
- **Knobs and handles** help us pull doors and lids.
- **Catches** keep doors and lids closed.

You can find hardware in more sizes and shapes than you can imagine at a home center. It also comes in a variety of materials, made for different purposes.

- **Iron and steel** are silvery and shiny. Most hardware is made of iron.
- **Iron coated with zinc** (called galvanized) resists rust, so it's good for outdoor projects.
- **Brass** is a shiny yellow-colored metal used to make projects more attractive.

Butt hinge is made of brass

Strap hinge is made of galvanized iron

Safety catch is made of bright, nickel-plated steel

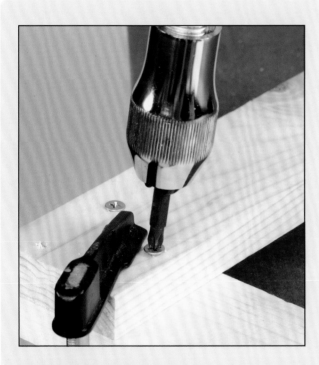

Glue and Screws

When you want to make something that is really really strong, use glue along with construction screws. Spread glue on both surfaces. Clamp the parts together. Then with the clamps in place, drill pilot holes and drive three or four wood screws through one piece into the other. It'll never come apart.

Power Drive

We use a brace with a screwdriver bit when we are driving a lot of screws for a large project, and when we are driving screws into hard wood. The brace has so much leverage you can twist the head right off the screw. Try it in scrap wood to learn how much power the brace has. It's very difficult to remove a screw with a broken head, but you can do it with locking pliers.

Paint and Varnish

Paint and varnish protect wood and make it easy to clean. Here's a quick list of three common finishes:

- **Paint** colors the wood and hides the wood figure. You can apply a coat of clear varnish after the paint dries for a glossy finish.
- **Varnish** lets the figure show through without adding color.
- **Stain** colors the wood without hiding the grain. You can apply a coat of clear varnish after the stain dries to protect a project.

For great colors on your wood projects, acrylic paint is best. Craft supply stores sell it as a liquid in little plastic bottles. You'll find dozens of colors you can mix together to get even more colors. Acrylic paints are water-based so there are no harmful fumes. They are easy to find, look terrific, dry quickly, last a long time, and don't cost much. Acrylics also allow you to add sharp-looking details, like stripes or lettering, after the paint has dried overnight (see the "Wishbone Racer" project on page 64).

You can also use water-based house paint and decorative enamels on woodworking projects, but they are harder to work with than craft acrylics. Oil-based paints and spray paints are messy and smelly, and some people are allergic to the fumes. If you do need to use paint in a spray can, use it outdoors and be sure to wear goggles and gloves.

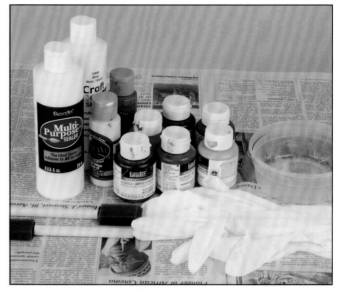

Color your wood projects with acrylic paint, which comes in small inexpensive bottles. Wear gloves, use disposable foam brushes, and protect the work table with newspaper.

Paint, stain, and varnish change the apperance of the wood.

| Bare wood | Water-based varnish | Antique pine stain | Acrylic paint | Acrylic paint with a varnish topcoat |

Skills:

Painting

Paint covers and dries better if you apply two or three thin coats rather than one thick coat. The first coat should be thinner than the topcoats so it sinks into the wood and grips better. Thin it by adding a small amount of water—about 1/10 to 1/5 of the amount of paint in your container. If you use a small deli container, one tablespoon of water is about right for half of the container. Use a clean stick to stir the mixture well before applying it.

Handling Paint

Paint, or any finish for that matter, can be very messy, and it doesn't just stick to wood. It sticks to people, too! So wear disposable rubber gloves, old clothes, and safety goggles when painting or finishing.

Clean small plastic deli containers or cat food cans make great containers for paint. Carefully filling one of these with paint until it's about half full will let you thin or mix paint colors without affecting your main supply. Replace the caps and lids on all of your cans and bottles, and keep them tightly closed so the paint won't dry out. Don't pour any leftover thinned or mixed paints back into the original containers. Instead, let it

dry out in the container and then discard it in the household trash.

To make cleaning up faster and easier, spread newspaper on the worktable before you start to paint and use disposable brushes. After you've finished painting, roll up the mess and throw it all away.

1

Preparing to Paint. Brush all the sanding dust off your project. Lay out all of your tools and supplies, including newspaper for your work surface. Don't forget to put on your safety goggles and rubber gloves. Thin and mix any paints as needed.

2

Applying Paint. Use a disposable foam brush to apply paint to your project. First brush it onto the wood in all directions. Then, smooth it out by brushing lightly in the same direction as the wood grain.

3

Paint It All. Paint the back and edges of your project first and let them dry. Then, paint the front. If you are in a hurry, you can prop the wet side on scraps of wood while you paint the top.

Chapter 3

Tools

You don't need a closet full of tools to begin working with wood, but you do need the right tools. The kit of hand tools shown here is all you'll need for the projects in this book and many other projects as well.

You probably have many of these tools at home already, so take a good look around. Gather up what you do find and put them all together. Then, clean them up to get them ready for use (see "Cleaning Up" below). If the tools you found belong to another family member, ask permission before you use them. Any tools you're missing can be purchased new at a hardware store or home center. You might also find low-cost tools for sale at flea markets or yard sales.

Cleaning Up

Cleaning up your tools and work area are a lot easier if you do it as you go along.

Here's a quick list to keep in mind:

- Sweep up the sawdust and dump it in the trash.
- Sort through your wood scraps and throw away any pieces smaller than your hand.
- Store pieces larger than your hand in a cardboard box for future use. You never know what you might be able to use later.
- Wipe wood chips and sawdust off your tools with a soft rag. To prevent rust, put a few drops of machine oil on the rag and wipe the metal with it. If rust has already formed, scrub the tool with steel wool and a little oil. Then, wipe it dry.
- Always keep a trash bin nearby and dump it regularly.

Safety Tools

Tools are sharp and wood is hard. Your body is soft and vulnerable in comparison! Protect yourself from injury whenever you do any woodworking. Obey all safety rules and stay focused on what you are doing and how you are doing it.

Eyes and Ears

Wear eye protection—either safety glasses or shop goggles—whenever you are in the workshop. The ones with side shields work best. If you wear eyeglasses, get safety goggles that fit over them. You won't need hearing protection with hand tools.

Hair

Put long hair up under a hat or tie it back whenever you are in the workshop. You don't want it tangled up in an eggbeater drill or dipped in glue.

Hands

Wear leather work gloves for handling rough wood or steel wool. When painting or finishing, slip on disposable rubber gloves.

Feet

Always wear sneakers or work boots in the workshop. *Do not wear sandals.* They don't provide enough protection. Imagine dropping a hammer on a bare toe!

Nose and Lungs

Disposable face masks, often called dust masks, help protect you from breathing in tiny particles of wood.

Clamping for Safety

Using clamps (page 24) or a vise (page 41) to secure your work is the simplest, best way to avoid getting hurt while woodworking. It frees both your hands for using tools and keeps them on tool handles, not near sharp edges. Inexperienced craftsmen sometimes try to hold the wood in one hand while using a tool with the other. This is a sure-fire way to get hurt. If the wood moves even a little bit and the tool slips, the hand holding the wood is going to get cut!

Clamps

Clamps hold wood still while you work on it. They can secure one piece of wood to the worktable or hold two pieces of wood together while glue dries. The kind of clamp you choose depends on your project and material. Clamps for woodworking come with sliding jaws so they securely tighten onto different-size woodworking projects.

Skills:

Clamping

A quick-set clamp with a sliding jaw is easy to use once you know the trick! You must first hold the fixed jaw in place and then put the movable jaw in position.

1 **Open the Clamp.** Turn the screw handle so the round clamp pad is close to the jaw. This gives you plenty of room to adjust the clamp.

2 **Plant the Fixed Jaw.** Hold the fixed jaw of the clamp steady and flat against the work.

3 **Set the Clamp.** Slide the movable jaw along the clamp bar until the pad rests flat on the wood. Then, tighten the clamp handle.

Coping Saw

A coping saw is a great tool for cutting curved parts. It has a narrow, easy-to-replace blade that fits inside a metal frame. Twisting the handle tightens and loosens the blade. For sawing pine planks, use blades with 10 or 15 teeth per inch (TPI). For thin material, such as ⅛" (0.3cm) plywood, blades with 20 TPI are better. The blade should be turned so the teeth point toward the handle. The saw cuts on the pull stroke.

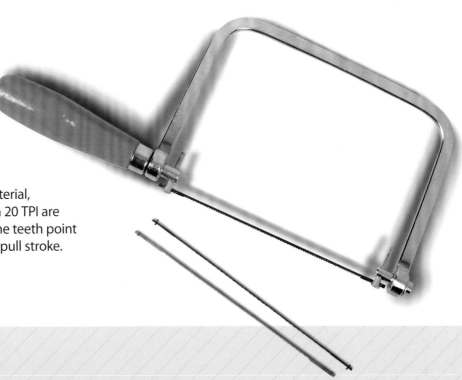

Skills:

Sawing Curves

Cutting curves with a coping saw is easy to do once you learn the techniques. First, keep the blade square to the wood's surface. If you don't, the sawn edge will slant and you'll have to sand forever to fix it. Second, practice turning the blade in the handle to get the best sawing angle.

1

Start the Saw. First draw your guideline and clamp the wood upright in the vise. Then, with both hands holding the coping saw, start making short, light cuts.

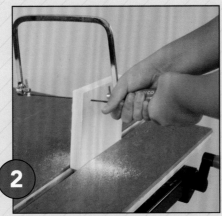

2

Follow the Guideline. Once the blade is into the wood, use the full length of the blade as you steer the saw along your guideline. Remember, the saw cuts on the pull stroke.

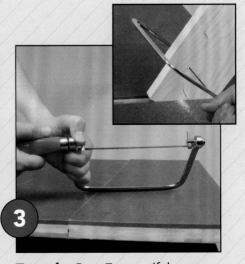

3

Turn the Saw Frame. If the saw frame bangs into the wood, loosen the handle and turn the blade so it clears. Then, tighten the handle again. Keep the blade clamps in line with each other.

Drill and Bits

The eggbeater drill is used to make little holes up to ¼" (0.5cm) diameter. The bit-brace makes larger holes using auger bits or an expansion bit.

Both kinds of drills have a chuck that holds the drill bit. A chuck is a sleeve you turn to open and close the jaws inside.

You need both hands to work the drill, so always clamp the workpiece to the bench or trap it in a vise. Clamp it onto a piece of scrap wood so the drill won't tear the wood as it chews through the back.

To work either kind of drill, press and guide the handle with one hand, while turning the crank with the other hand. With a bit brace, you can get additional help by using your head—literally! Just press your forehead onto the hand that's holding the handle of the drill. Your head and body will act as a brace to keep the tool steady, as shown in "Skills: Drilling Holes" on page 27.

Power Tools

You should learn to ride a bicycle before you hop on a motorcycle, right? Well, you also need to learn to work with hand tools before you use power tools. Before long, you'll be ready for a cordless electric drill, a portable saber saw, and a random-orbit sander. These three tools will open up a whole new set of projects for you to tackle.

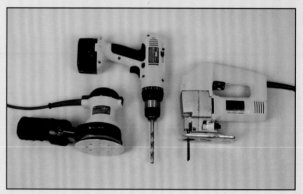

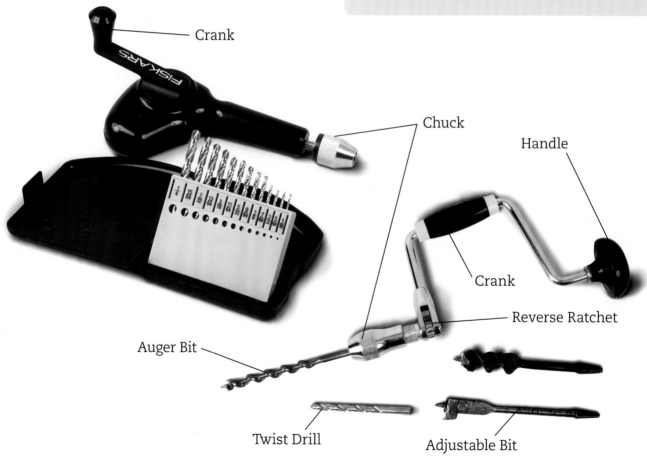

Crank

Chuck

Handle

Crank

Reverse Ratchet

Auger Bit

Twist Drill

Adjustable Bit

Skills:

Drilling Holes

Let's practice making true holes with the brace and bit. A true hole doesn't slant—it's square to the surface of the wood. Firmly clamp the wood you are drilling onto a piece of scrap wood on the worktable.

Buddy Tip

If you are working with a buddy, ask him to eyeball the drill against the square. Have him move around, while you use the drill, to make sure it stays true in all directions.

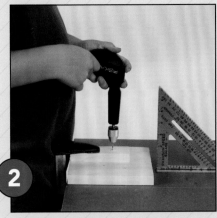

1

Chuck the Bit. Choose a drill bit that is the exact size of the hole you want. Put the bit all the way into the chuck and tighten it as hard as you can.

2

Align the Drill. Mark the placement of the center of the hole with the awl or center punch. Put the point of the drill bit on the center mark, and then use the speed square to line it up.

3

Drill the Hole. Turn the drill crank to make the drill bite into the wood. It will start to cut and lift the chips of wood out of the hole. Brace your hand holding the drill with your forehead.

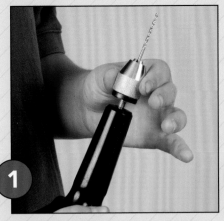

4

Drilling Practice. For practice, drill holes in a block to hold small hand tools. Saw a piece of 2x4 to fit inside your tool tote (page 53). Draw a grid on the wood and drill a ⁵⁄₁₆" (0.8cm) hole at each crossing.

Drill Bits

Twist drills can make holes in wood, plastic, and metal. They are sized in sixty-fourths and thirty-seconds of an inch and usually come as a set like the one shown at right. Store the drills in the drill case so you know the size of each one. (The case has holes to test the size of nails and screws, too.) These twist drills can also be used in an electric drill.

For larger holes, up to 1" (2.5cm) in diameter, use auger bits. Auger bits are sized in sixteenths of an inch, so a No. 8 bit drills an ⁸⁄₁₆" hole, or ½" (1.5cm). Auger bits cannot be used in an electric drill.

For holes larger than 1" (2.5cm), use an expansion bit like the one shown at left. It has an adjustable cutter; set it to the exact size you need. Test the size in scrap wood before you drill your project.

Hammer

As you probably already know, we use hammers to drive nails into wood, and there are many different kinds of hammers. For woodworking, choose a claw hammer, also called a carpenter's hammer. It should have a curved claw, not a straight one, for pulling nails out of wood.

Grip the hammer by its handle and swing it at a piece of wood. If your hand slides toward the head of the hammer, or you need two hands to swing it, the hammer is too heavy for you. A 10-ounce, 14-ounce, or 18-ounce hammer is usually heavy enough. By comparison, a professional builder uses a 28-ounce framing hammer and swings it all day long!

You can practice swinging your hammer at a chunk 2x4. First, clamp the wood to the worktable. Then, holding the grip part of the handle, swing the hammer from your elbow, keeping your wrist locked. See if you can make nice, round dents, sometimes called elephant tracks, in the wood.

Now, you are ready to practice driving 1½" (4cm) box nails into the wood. Drive at least five nails. Count how many blows you need to hammer a nail all the way in. See what happens if you drive the nail close to the edge of the wood—it might split.

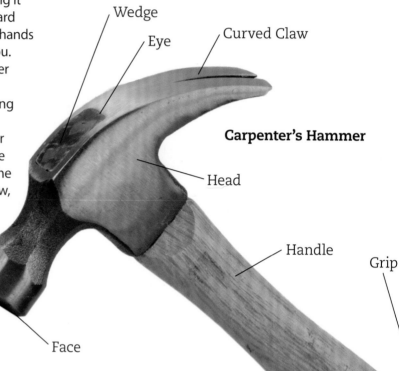

Wedge

Eye

Curved Claw

Carpenter's Hammer

Head

Handle

Grip

Face

Framing hammer has a straight claw

Mechanic's hammer is also called a ball-peen hammer

Skills:

How to Hammer a Nail

It is time to learn how to drive a nail straight and all the way into the wood. Don't use nails so long that their points stick out the other side. Try to do a neat job. For this exercise, you'll use one piece of wood to draw a nailing line on the other, start the nails into the first piece, clamp the two pieces together, and then drive the nails into the second piece. Use two or three nails. More nails will not do a better job; they will just weaken the wood.

How to Not Hit Your Fingers

Are you afraid of hitting your fingers when you hammer? That's okay. Nobody likes a blue thumb! You can start your nail by holding it in place with pliers instead of your fingers, until your aim improves.

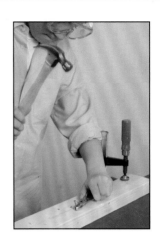

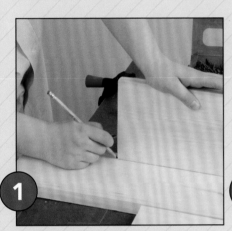

1

Draw Nailing Lines. Hold the two pieces of wood together and draw a nailing line. Draw three X's for three nails. Remember, nails placed too close to the corners or edges might split the wood.

2

Start the Nails. Hold the nail against the wood with your fingers. Use light hammer taps to start it. Knock in the nail enough that it's straight and secure but not driven through the piece.

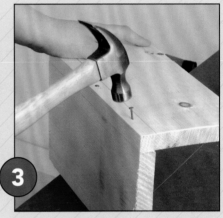

3

Hammer the Nails. Clamp or hold the pieces together, and hammer the first nail all the way in. Check to be sure the pieces are still lined up where you want them to be before you drive in the other nails.

Pulling Nails

If a nail bends or goes sideways, stop and pull it out with the hammer claw. Do this when it first starts to bend. Do not pound it down flat. After you remove it, throw the bent nail away. You can't really straighten a bent nail. It will just bend again.

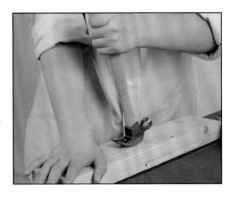

Knife

We use a small, sharp knife to sharpen pencils, make layout lines, and to whittle softwoods like pine. A sharp knife is safer than a dull one. One way to have a sharp knife all the time is to use one with disposable blades, or breakaway blades, right. The yellow knife has interchangeable blades. The wood-handled one at the right is for whittling.

Whittling

When you want to sharpen a pencil or change the shape of a piece of wood, you can do it with a small sharp knife. When you remove a chip of wood at a time with a knife, it's called whittling. Whittlers use several different knife grips, each designed to help you cut the wood and not yourself.

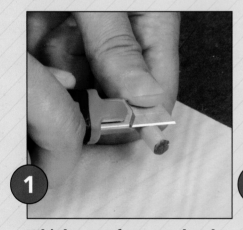

1

Whittle away from your hand. Hold the pencil in one hand, the point aimed away from your body. Hold the knife in your other hand, the edge away from you. Always whittle away from your fingers, never toward them.

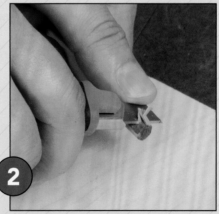

2

Controlled cut. Press the knife blade into the wood with your thumb. This grip gives you a lot of control and cutting power.

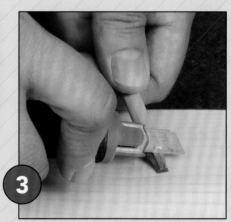

3

Brace the wood. When you want to remove a lot of wood, brace the workpiece on the worktable. Hold the knife in your fist and power it at a shallow angle down the wood.

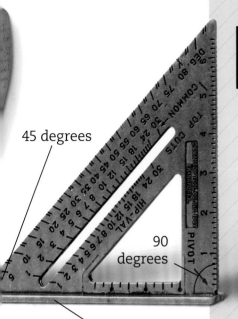

45 degrees

90 degrees

Fence

Speed Square

A speed square is a metal or plastic triangle with an additional strip of metal, called a fence, fastened to one edge. Because it is a right triangle, it is square at one corner. Speed squares help you draw square lines across wood so you can make sure your projects fit neatly together and stand up straight. **Note:** If you ever need to know whether something is square and you don't have a speed square handy, use the corner of a CD case.

A 7" (18cm) speed square is big enough for small projects, but most carpenters prefer the 12" (30.5cm) size. Notice that this square has angle markings on its face. Carpenters use these markings to build roofs on houses.

Skills:

How to Measure and Mark

The most common layout task is marking a long board where you intend to saw off a short one. The short board should be just the right length and must have square ends.

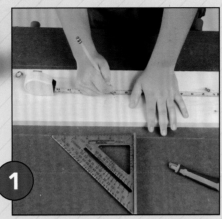

1 **Measure.** Hook the tape measure over one end of the board and pull it along the wood. Make a small pencil mark on the wood at the end of the correct length. Carefully let the tape measure go back into its case.

2 **Draw a Square Line.** Hold the fence of the speed square tight against the edge of the wood with one hand, slide it up to your measured mark, and then draw a line along the edge of the square.

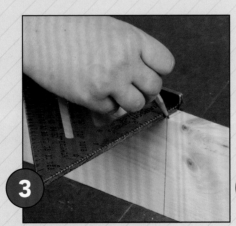

3 **Extend the Square Line.** Use the speed square to extend the line across both edges and the back of the wood. This will give you a sawing guide all the way around.

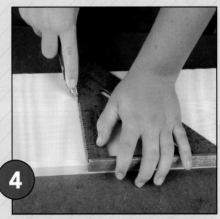

4 **Knife the Line.** For a really clean saw cut without splinters, draw the tip of your knife along the square. Doing so will deepen the pencil line and cut the fibers at the surface.

Measuring and Marking Tools

Measuring and marking the wood accurately is important if you want your project to have neatly fitting parts. A tape measure is used to mark out dimensions, and a speed square is used to mark right angles for making square crosscuts. To draw long straight lines, measure and mark in two places. Connect the marks by drawing along a ruler or the edge of another board. For circles, use a compass or trace a round object that's about the size you want.

Awl

Use an awl for marking the centers of holes before you drill, starting small nails and screws without drilling pilot holes, and scratching layout lines onto wood, metals, and plastics. To make a deep mark, tap the awl with the heel of your hand or hit it lightly with a hammer.

Tape Measure

A tape measure is a long ribbon of flexible steel that can roll back up inside its case. This important tool has large marks showing the inches and smaller marks showing sixteenths and thirty-seconds of an inch. Most tape measures have additional red marks every sixteen inches that carpenters use—2x4s inside walls are 16" (40.5cm) apart. For the projects in this book, you'll need a standard 12' long, half-inch wide tape measure.

Make Them Match

For most woodworking projects, exact size doesn't matter as much as having one part match another. Hold one part against the other. Draw a line along it to transfer edges and shapes.

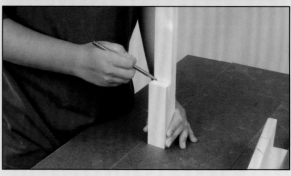

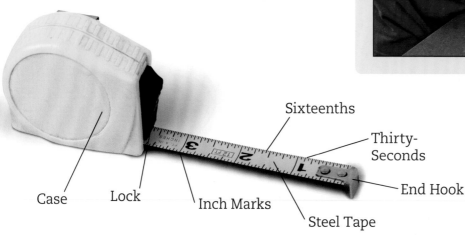

Sixteenths

Thirty-Seconds

End Hook

Case

Lock

Inch Marks

Steel Tape

Nail Set

Even though a finishing nail has a small head, you can still see it on the wood's surface. A nail set will punch the tiny head below the surface. Then, you can hide it completely by filling the little hole, or dimple, in the wood with wood dough or putty.

Pliers

Pliers allow you to get a good grip on wire, nails, and screws for many different purposes. There are pliers for electrical work, welding, or making jewelry. Pliers can hold a small nail while you hammer it in (page 29) to protect your fingers. Locking pliers can pull a nail or twist a broken screw out of the wood. Some pliers even include sharp edges for cutting wire. You will need wire-cutting pliers for the rubber-band shooter project later in this book (page 79).

Rasp

A rasp is a bar of steel covered with sharp little teeth. It can remove wood just like coarse sandpaper. Rasps often have different shapes. A half-round rasp, shaped like a half moon, has both a flat side and a curved side. Wood must be sanded smooth with medium and fine sandpaper after rasping.

Rasps and files have a sharp point, the tang, where the handle fits. Never use a rasp with a bare tang and no handle. If the rasp catches on the wood, the tang might go into your hand.

Nail set drives finishing nail head below the wood's surface

Pliers firmly grip metal parts

Rasp quickly removes rough saw marks from wood

Miter Box

A miter box helps you crosscut pieces of wood by holding the work steady and guiding the saw. They are available in wood or plastic. Use your toolbox saw with a wooden one; use a backsaw with a plastic one. Most boxes fit wood up to 4" (10cm) wide. They saw both square crosscuts and 45-degree angles, which are often called miters.

Woodworkers use miters to join the corners of frames and boxes because their appearance is symmetrical and neat. Although we usually think of miters as being 45 degrees, a miter is really any angle divided exactly in half.

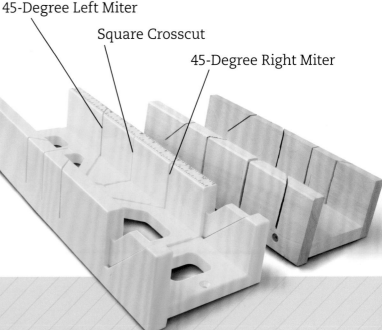

45-Degree Left Miter

Square Crosscut

45-Degree Right Miter

Skills:

Crosscutting with the Miter Box

Place the miter box on the worktable with its front edge hooked over the edge of the table. If the box is new, deepen the cuts down to the bottom of the box before sawing any project wood. Use the speed square to make layout lines on the wood.

(1) Load the Box. Brush any sawdust out of the box. Place the project wood in it. Slide the layout line to the crosscut slot at the back of the box. Pay attention to which side of the line you want to cut. Clamp the wood in place.

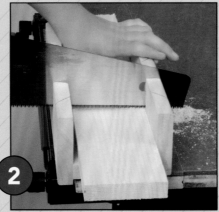

(2) Start the Cut. Fit the saw into the crosscut slot. Tilt it to start cutting at the far edge of the workpiece. Start cutting the wood with short strokes, without applying any downward pressure. You will see the saw enter the wood at the back of the box.

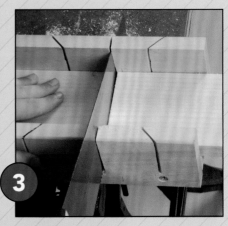

(3) Extend the Cut. Once the saw starts cutting, lengthen your stroke, applying a little downward pressure. Lower the saw handle so the teeth are level with the box bottom. Saw until the wood breaks free. If you saw into the bottom of the box, it's not a problem.

Tape Trick

Pull your measuring tape about 20 inches (50cm) out of its case and hold it straight up. No problemo, right? Now pull out some more tape. See how much tape you can make stand straight up. How about 4 feet? Now try for 6 feet…

Teeth per inch

Saws with many TPI are for smooth cuts and thin materials. Saws with few teeth per inch are for rough cuts and thick materials. Some saws are marked in TPI, while others are marked in points per inch (PPI). A saw with 10 teeth has 11 points. There's always one more point than teeth.

Do Branches get Higher?

Suppose you hung a swing from a low branch on a maple tree. If you left for 20 years and then returned, do you think the swing would be any higher off the ground?

   The answer is no. Trees grow taller at the top, and the trunk gets thicker as the tree gets older, but the trunk itself doesn't get taller and branches don't get any higher off the ground.

More Useful Supplies

Fine steel wool. Scrub with fine steel wool to smooth varnish between coats, and to remove rust and dirt from old tools. Wear work gloves when using steel wool.

Household oil. A small can of oil will lubricate hinges and hardware so they work well, and will help you clean dirt and rust off old tools.

Sanding Block

To save wear and tear on your fingers and get the most out of sandpaper, use a hard rubber sanding block. The block keeps the sandpaper tight and flat and gives you something to grip. Fold and tear the sheets into strips or squares to fit the sanding block. The rubber sanding block shown at right uses quarter-sheets of sandpaper that clip onto sharp points inside the block. Some sanding blocks have hook-and-loop backing. They are used for sanding between coats of finish, not for shaping wood.

Fit your block with coarse sandpaper to make wood flat, to smooth out marks and bumps left by a saw, and to change the shape of corners and edges. Use medium sandpaper to smooth wood and remove splinters. Fine sandpaper prepares wood for finishing with paint and varnish and is used between coats of finish.

Even if wood looks clean and new, it will look even better after you rub it with sandpaper. Sanding is usually easier if you do it before the pieces are assembled. You won't be able to get at the inside corners of an assembled piece.

Each sanding grit or grade (coarse, medium, fine, etc.) removes the scratches left by the one before. Though it's tempting to start with fine sandpaper, or to jump directly from coarse to fine, you will do less work if you just stick with the coarse-medium-fine sequence (see page 14). Remember to brush or vacuum up the sanding dust when you're finished.

To attach a strip of sandpaper to a rubber sanding block, lift the end flap and press the paper onto the points inside.

Skills:

Sanding

Always sand flat wood surfaces in the direction of the wood grain, never across it. Corners can be shaped by sanding with the block held at an angle to the wood. To smooth rough-sawn edges, place the wood in a vise and hold the block crosswise, using both hands.

Sanding Protection

Sawdust in your eyes really hurts, so wear your safety goggles when sanding wood. Especially if you are using an electric sander, keep the fine wood dust out of your mouth, nose, and lungs by wearing a dust mask, too.

1

Sand the Surface Smooth. Make the wood smooth by scrubbing it with sandpaper on the sanding block. Work in the same direction as the wood grain.

2

Sand the Edges. Mount the wood in a vise. To remove deep saw marks and make an edge flat, use both hands to press hard while you work the block back and forth across the wood.

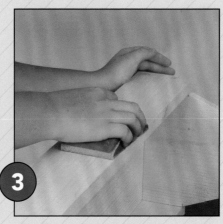

3

Sand the Corners Hand-Friendly. Sand the sharp edges and corners. You can sand a little to remove splinters, or a lot to shape the wood.

Sanding Practice

Let's practice sanding corners and edges. Put 100-grit sandpaper on the sanding block. Then, saw an 8" (20.5cm)-long piece of 1x6 wood to 5" (12.5cm) wide. Next, sand the sawn edge as smooth and flat as the opposite edge. Don't forget to put the wood in the vise or clamp it to the worktable. Hold the block in two hands, as in Step 2, above.

Now, sand three of the block's four long corners. Leave one edge alone. Sand the second edge to take the sharpness off. Sand the third edge flat, all the way along: a chamfer. Then, sand the last edge until it's about as round as a pencil: a roundover. Do the same with three of the four crossways edges. Check your work and compare the four edges. How did you do? Which edge do you like best? If you're not happy with your work, just try it again.

Saw

There are many kinds of saws. Some are made for crosscutting, while others are made for ripping wood lengthwise. For small projects like the ones in this book, choose a 15" (38cm) toolbox-style saw with 12 TPI. This type of saw has long, sharp teeth that can crosscut and rip, making it a good general-purpose tool. Like most handsaws, the toolbox-style saw cuts on the push stroke.

Sawing Practice

Let's practice making crosscuts in a 1x6. First, use the speed square to draw three guide lines 2" (5cm) apart. Extend the lines onto the edges of the board. Clamp the board in the vise and saw the first line, as explained in "Sawing Wood." You don't have to press hard to make the saw work.

If the saw wanders off the line, don't worry about it. Complete the cut without trying to steer the saw, since steering doesn't work. If you try to steer the saw, the wandering might get worse or the saw might bind and not saw at all.

Check the piece you cut off with the speed square to see how straight your cut was. Is it square to the surface? Now try again to see if you can do even better.

Try different positions too. Your arm has a natural stroke. You can improve your sawing ability by changing both where you stand and how you hold the saw at the start of the cut.

If your saw comes with a strip of plastic on the blade, keep it. It will protect the sharp saw teeth from damage if they bang into other tools in your toolbox.

Toolbox-style saws have teeth that crosscut and rip.

Skills:

Sawing Wood

Most of the sawing for your projects in this book will be crosscutting. Before you begin, draw guidelines as shown on page 31, extending them around the edges of the wood. The lines will help you make a square cut.

Crosscutting can be done two different ways: with the wood held up on edge in a vise or with the wood lying flat on the table. Try both ways to learn which one is more comfortable for you. If you are sawing slanted lines, hold the wood upright in the vise with the layout line as close to vertical as possible. Remember to always clamp the work so it can't move around.

Crosscutting and Ripping

Crosscutting means sawing the wood across its width, which makes boards shorter. Ripping means sawing wood along its length, which makes boards narrower.

 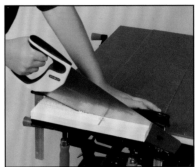

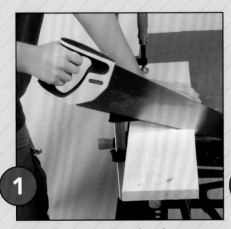

1

Start the Saw. Stand with your sawing arm in line with the cut. Place your other hand on the wood. Make short, light strokes to break the corner and get the teeth into the wood.

2

Saw the Line. Keep the saw square to the wood. Make longer strokes to extend the cut all the way along the line. Push the saw, but don't try to steer it. If it starts going the wrong way, turn the wood over and start again from the other edge.

3

Catch the Falling Wood. Slow down as you reach the end of the cut and make short, light strokes. Reach over with your other hand to support the cut-off piece, so it doesn't fall and splinter.

Screwdrivers

Screwdrivers come in many types and sizes to turn screws into wood. Each different type or shape fits a certain kind of screw head. Most of the screws you will use can be driven with a No. 2 screwdriver. You will need straight screwdrivers for straight-slot screws and Phillips, or cross-drive, screwdrivers for crosshead screws.

Driving Screws

Practice drilling pilot holes and driving screws straight in the wood. You'll use screws to attach hardware and to strengthen joints.

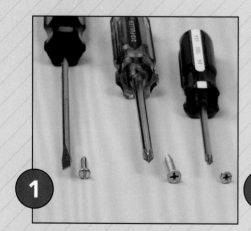

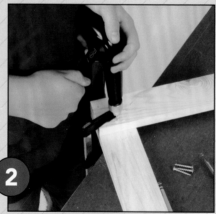

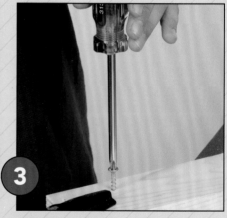

1 **Match Screwdriver and Screw.** Check that your screwdriver matches the screw head. Fit the screwdriver into the screw slot. It should be a snug fit. If it's too loose, it will probably slip.

2 **Drill a Pilot Hole.** Drill a pilot hole using the eggbeater drill and a bit that is smaller than the screw. For flathead screws, drill a shallow countersink to fit the screw head.

3 **Drive the Screw.** Fit the screwdriver into the screw head and twist the screw into the wood. Keep the screwdriver and screw in a straight line or the screw will slip. Drive the screw down nice and tight.

Workbench and Vise

Your work area should be set up just for you and include a workbench and vise. The workbench should be a sturdy table that will not move around when you pound on it. If you don't already have something like that, you can build your own workbench or buy a worktable, such as the Workmate®, which comes with a built-in vise.

A vise is a large clamp used for holding your project pieces. If you are right-handed, the vise should be near the right-hand end of the bench. If you are left-handed, it should be at the left. You can position a clamp-on vise anywhere you like.

Vises for woodworking have wide jaws with wooden faces so they don't damage the work. Vises for metalworking are smaller with small jaws and rough metal faces to grip hard iron and steel. If you do not have a vise, you can use clamps for these projects instead (page 24).

The height of a workbench is important. Stand up straight with your arms at your sides. Now bend your wrist to hold your hand out flat. The distance from your hand to the floor is the right height for your workbench. Up to 3" (7.5cm) higher or lower is okay too.

Chapter 4

Projects

Project: Trophy Base

All of us are proud of the awards and certificates we earn, and it's fun to display them for everyone to see. This project will provide a nice base, or plinth, for those trophies, and it's something else you'll be proud to show. To complete the project, you'll need to practice the measuring and marking skills (page 31), sawing (page 39), sanding (page 37), and nailing (page 29).

The plinth may be painted (see "Painting Instructions," page 21), or sanded and left unfinished. You might also choose to glue your trophy onto the plinth using 5-minute epoxy.

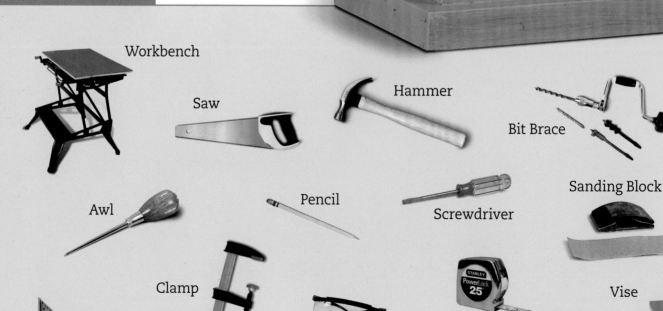

TOOLS

Workbench

Saw

Hammer

Bit Brace

Awl

Pencil

Screwdriver

Sanding Block

Clamp

Vise

Square

Safety Glasses

Tape Measure

Plans: **How the Trophy Base Goes Together**

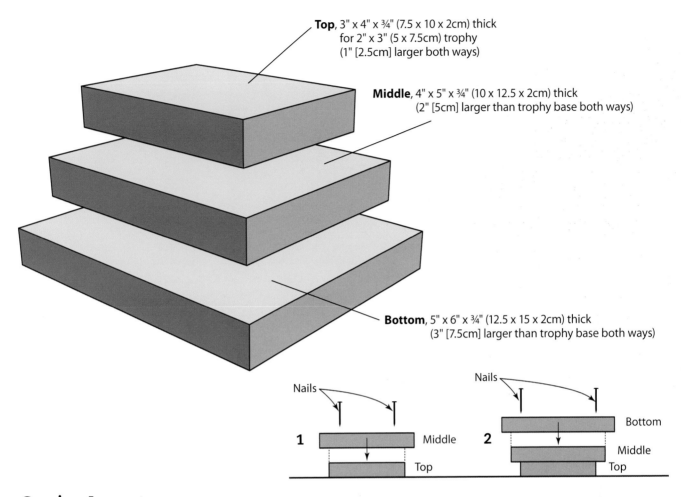

Top, 3" x 4" x ¾" (7.5 x 10 x 2cm) thick
for 2" x 3" (5 x 7.5cm) trophy
(1" [2.5cm] larger both ways)

Middle, 4" x 5" x ¾" (10 x 12.5 x 2cm) thick
(2" [5cm] larger than trophy base both ways)

Bottom, 5" x 6" x ¾" (12.5 x 15 x 2cm) thick
(3" [7.5cm] larger than trophy base both ways)

Nails

1 Middle · Top

Nails

2 Bottom · Middle · Top

Sawing Layout

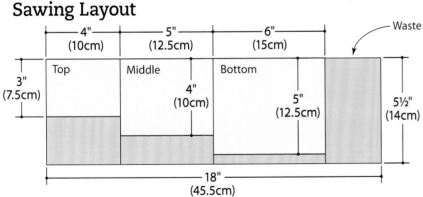

4" (10cm) · 5" (12.5cm) · 6" (15cm) · Waste

3" (7.5cm)

Top · Middle · Bottom

4" (10cm) · 5" (12.5cm) · 5½" (14cm)

18" (45.5cm)

Skills
- Measuring, page 31
- Sawing, page 39
- Sanding, page 37
- Miter Box, for square crosscuts, page 34
- Nailing, page 29

Lumber
- 1" x 6" x 18" (2.5 x 15 x 45.5cm) pine or cedar

Supplies
- 1¼" (3cm) finishing nails, 6
- 100-grit sandpaper, ¼ sheet
- 150-grit sandpaper, ¼ sheet
- Varnish or acrylic paints (optional)

Building: **Trophy Base**

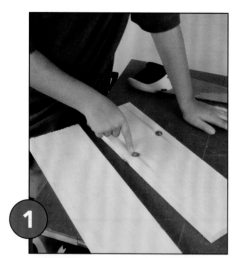

Choose the Wood. Choose smooth, clean wood without any knots or other defects. The plinth should call attention to your award, not to itself.

Draw Guidelines. Measure your trophy base and add 1" (2.5cm) to its length and width. With a tape measure, mark the dimensions on the wood. Extend the marks using the speed square.

Crosscut the Wood. Clamp the wood to the worktable and make the saw cuts across the wood. If the wood fits into your miter box, use it to make the cuts.

Sawing Safely

When sawing, remember to always clamp wood to the worktable or hold it firmly in a vise. Don't try to hold the wood still with one hand and saw with the other—you'll probably cut yourself. Using a vise allows you to hold the handsaw with two hands. If sawing one-handed is more comfortable, you can rest your other hand on the wood at least 6" (15cm) away from the cutting action, but still keep the wood clamped down good and tight.

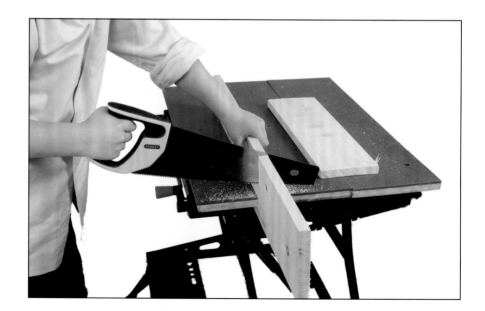

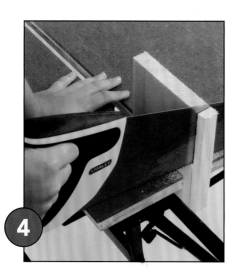

4

Rip the Wood. Now, clamp the wood to the worktable and make your rip cuts. Ripping is easier when the wood is held upright in a vise.

5

Sand the Wood Smooth. Clamp the wood in the vise with one edge up. Remove saw marks from the edge with the sanding block and 100-grit sandpaper. Smooth the edges on all pieces.

6

Sand the Corners. Holding the sanding block at an angle, sand off the sharp corners of the wood. Spend the same amount of time on each, so the corners and edges all look the same.

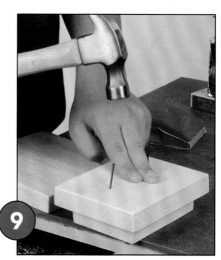

7

Sand the Wood Smooth. Change to 150-grit sandpaper. Sand the top and bottom surfaces of the blocks just enough to remove pencil marks and make the wood feel really smooth.

8

Make Assembly Marks. Put the trophy in place so you can center each piece on the plinth. Lightly outline each piece on the one below.

9

Nail the Pieces Together. Use two or three 1¼" (3cm) finishing nails for each connection. First, nail through the middle piece into the top piece. Then, nail through the bottom piece into the middle piece.

Project: Display Pedestal

Here is a pedestal for a wooden car, or for anything else that you want to display. Don't glue your car to the display pedestal. There's a trophy display base in the previous project, and later on we'll make a frame that can be used for photos, artwork, or award certificates.

To complete this project, you'll need to practice measuring and marking, sawing, nailing the posts subassembly together, then gluing and clamping the posts subassembly to the base.

TOOLS

 Hammer

 Square

Pencil

Miter Box

Workbench

 Tape Measure

Clamp

Saw

Safety Glasses

Sanding Block

Plans: **How the Display Pedestal Goes Together**

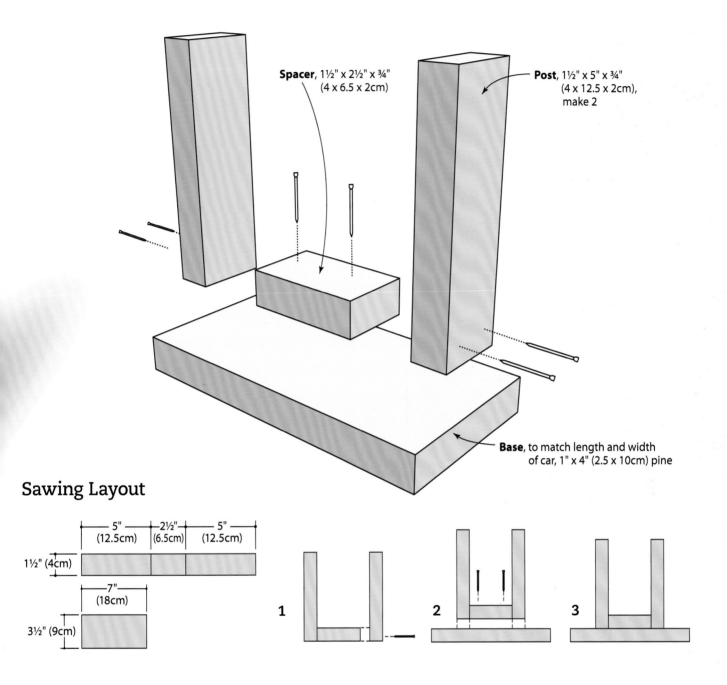

Spacer, 1½" x 2½" x ¾" (4 x 6.5 x 2cm)

Post, 1½" x 5" x ¾" (4 x 12.5 x 2cm), make 2

Base, to match length and width of car, 1" x 4" (2.5 x 10cm) pine

Sawing Layout

5" (12.5cm) — 2½" (6.5cm) — 5" (12.5cm)

1½" (4cm)

7" (18cm)

3½" (9cm)

1

2

3

Skills
- Measuring, page 31
- Sawing, page 39
- Sanding, page 37
- Nailing, page 29

Lumber
- 1" x 4" x 1' (2.5 x 10 x 30.5cm) pine
- 1" x 2" x 2' (2.5 x 5 x 61cm) pine

Supplies
- 100-grit sandpaper, ¼ sheet
- 150-grit sandpaper, ¼ sheet
- Nails
- Small paintbrush
- Wood glue

Building: **Display Pedestal**

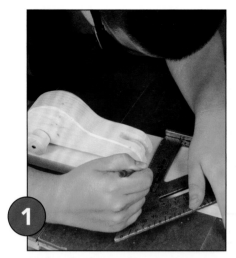

1

Make the base. Place your racing car on a length of 1x4 wood to mark its length. Use the square to extend this mark across the wood, then put it in the miter box and saw it to this length.

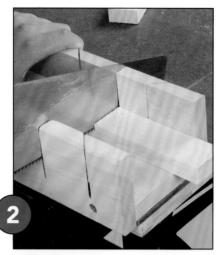

2

Make one post. Use the square to lay out the length of one post and the spacer. The precise length is up to you. Put the wood in the miter box and crosscut these two pieces.

3

Make the matching post. Use the first post as a guide for marking the length of the other. It's important they match, but not important how long they measure. Crosscut the second post.

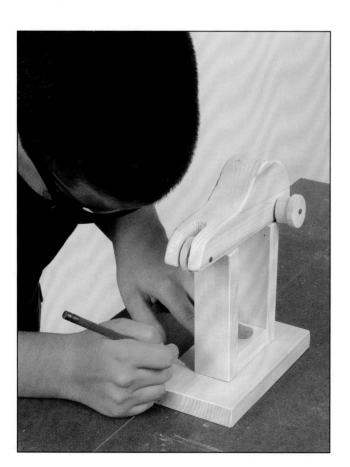

Assembly Marks

Always put your project parts together and have a good look before you join them with nails or glue. Arrange them to suit yourself—whatever looks best to you. Then record your choices by drawing small, L-shaped marks to show where everything fits. These lines are called "assembly marks."

4

Sand the wood. Follow the directions in steps 5, 6, and 7 in the previous project to sand all the wood smooth. Hold each post in the vise so you can sand the ends.

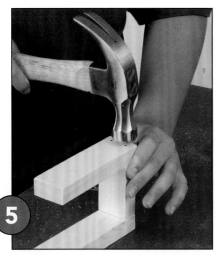

5

Nail posts to spacer. Start the nails with the posts flat on the worktable. Drive them almost all of the way through. Nail both posts to the spacer. Be sure the bottom is flat.

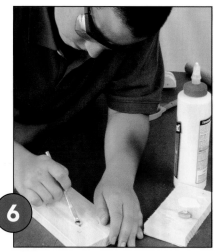

6

Join posts to base. Spread glue on base piece, inside your assembly marks. Squeeze a puddle of glue onto scrap wood and load your brush from it. Spread glue on the post assembly, too.

7

Clamp the parts. Clamp the post assembly onto the base piece. If there is any squeezed-out glue, wipe it off before it has time to dry.

Project: Desk Nameplate

This desk nameplate is quick and fun to create, and it makes a terrific gift for family members, teachers, or friends. You can leave the wood unfinished to show off the wood figure or paint it any color you choose. The desk nameplate shown was assembled and painted before the unfinished letters were glued onto it.

TOOLS

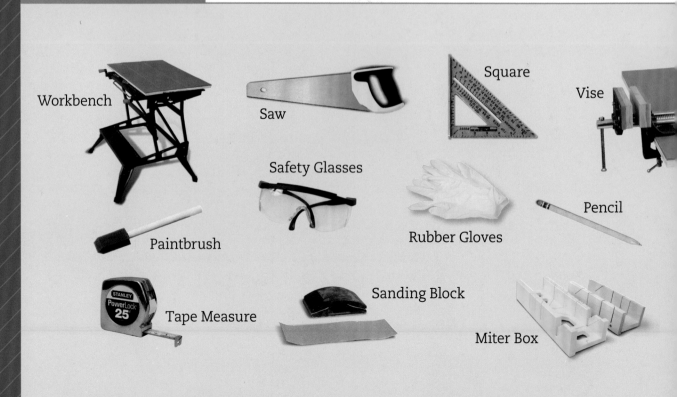

Workbench

Saw

Square

Vise

Safety Glasses

Rubber Gloves

Pencil

Paintbrush

Sanding Block

Tape Measure

Miter Box

Plans: **How the Desk Nameplate Goes Together**

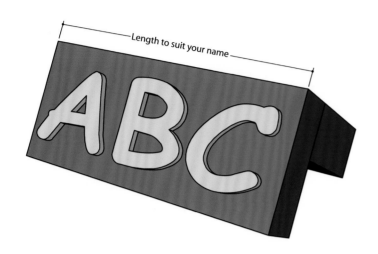

Length to suit your name

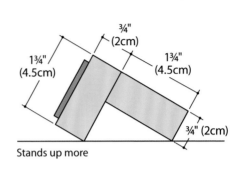

¾" (2cm)

1¾" (4.5cm)

1¾" (4.5cm)

¾" (2cm)

Stands up more

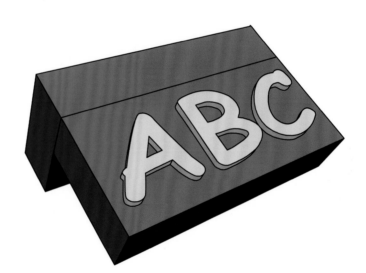

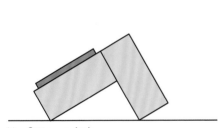

Lies flatter on desk

Skills
- Measuring, page 31
- Sawing, page 39
- Painting, page 21
- Gluing, page 16

Lumber
- 1" x 2" x 18" (2.5 x 5 x 45.5cm) pine
- Assorted letters from craft shop

Supplies
- Wood glue
- 150-grit sandpaper, 1 sheet
- Acrylic paints
- Small paintbrush

Building: Desk Nameplate

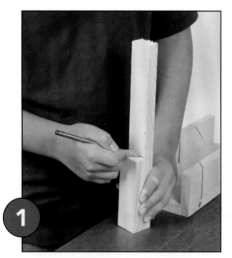

1

Saw the Wood. Line up the letters so they are close but not touching. Measure their length and add 1" (2.5cm). Crosscut one piece to that length. Then, mark and cut the second piece to match the first.

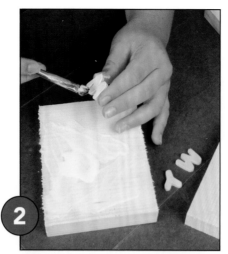

2

Glue the Letters. Brush glue on letters' backs and press them on the wood, keeping them even and straight. Clamp them or leave them flat until the glue dries. **Note:** If you want unfinished letters or letters a different color than the base, paint the base before gluing the letters.

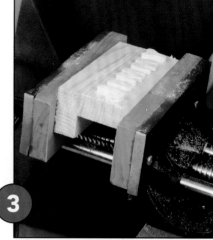

3

Glue the Wood. Glue the front piece to the back piece to form an L. Clamp the wood and let the glue dry. If excess glue dribbles, wipe it off immediately with a clean, damp rag or paper towel.

Find the Letters

The nameplate uses ⅛" (0.3cm) letters you can buy at a craft shop. They're usually sold in bags of about 300 assorted letters. If you want to saw the letters for yourself, see the "Keep Out Sign" project, page 74, for patterns and instructions.

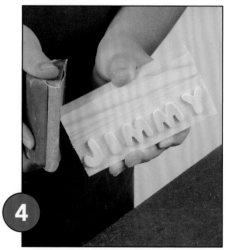

4

Sand and Paint. After the glue has dried, sand the corners of the nameplate and the surface where the two pieces of wood join. Then, paint the entire nameplate in whatever color you want.

Project: Tool Tote

This tote is handy because it keeps all of your tools in one place. It also protects them from damage and makes it easy to take your tools wherever your project might be. To do all of these things, the tote must be strong and needs a handle. That makes this project slightly more complicated.

Through this project, you'll learn how to draw square and angled guidelines, use a brace and bit to make the hole for the handle, and nail boxes together. Leave the tote unfinished or paint it any way you like.

This tote holds all the tools in Chapter 3, plus a few extra. To see how to mount the tote handle without drilling a large hole, see page 59.

TOOLS

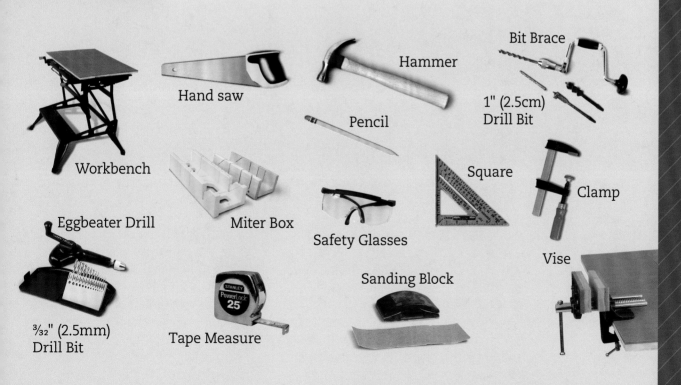

Workbench

Hand saw

Hammer

Pencil

Bit Brace

1" (2.5cm) Drill Bit

Square

Clamp

Eggbeater Drill

Miter Box

Safety Glasses

Vise

Sanding Block

³⁄₃₂" (2.5mm) Drill Bit

Tape Measure

Plans: **How the Tool Tote Goes Together**

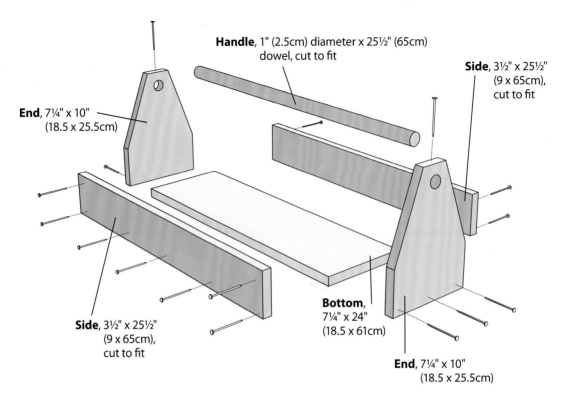

Handle, 1" (2.5cm) diameter x 25½" (65cm) dowel, cut to fit

Side, 3½" x 25½" (9 x 65cm), cut to fit

End, 7¼" x 10" (18.5 x 25.5cm)

Side, 3½" x 25½" (9 x 65cm), cut to fit

Bottom, 7¼" x 24" (18.5 x 61cm)

End, 7¼" x 10" (18.5 x 25.5cm)

Sawing Layout

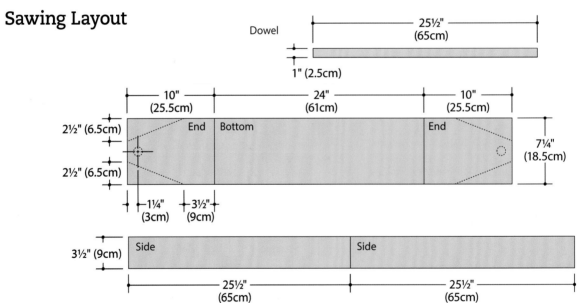

Dowel

25½" (65cm)

1" (2.5cm)

10" (25.5cm)   24" (61cm)   10" (25.5cm)

2½" (6.5cm)

End   Bottom   End

2½" (6.5cm)

7¼" (18.5cm)

1¼" (3cm)   3½" (9cm)

3½" (9cm)

Side   Side

25½" (65cm)   25½" (65cm)

Skills

- Measuring, page 31
- Drilling, page 27
- Sawing, page 39
- Sanding, page 37
- Nailing, page 29

Lumber

- 1" x 8" x 4' (2.5 x 20.5 x 122cm) pine
- 1" x 4" x 6' (2.5 x 10 x 183cm) pine
- 1" (2.5cm) poplar dowel

Note: Standard 1x8 pine lumber actually measures 7¼" (18.5cm) wide by ¾" (2cm) thick. 1x4 pine is 3½" (9cm) wide.

Supplies

- 1½" (4cm) galvanized finishing nails, 22
- 100-grit sandpaper, 1 sheet
- 150-grit sandpaper, 1 sheet
- 220-grit sandpaper, 1 sheet

Building: Tool Tote

1

Draw Guidelines. Lay a 1x8 plank on the worktable. Use a tape measure to mark and draw the layout lines all the way across the plank, as shown on page 54.

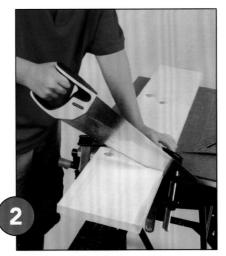

2

Crosscut the Wood. To saw the first line, clamp the wood to the worktable so that 1' (30.5cm) extends over the edge. Move and re-clamp the wood to make each crosscut.

3

Lay Out the Ends. Mark the angles on the end pieces. They start 3½" (9cm) from the bottom and end 1⅛" (3cm) from either side of the board's center at the top. Find and mark the center for the handle hole.

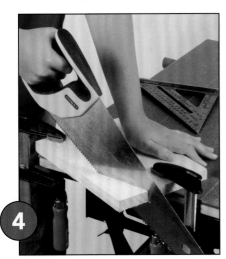

4

Saw the Angles. Clamp the wood to the worktable, with the layout line extending past the table's edge. Hold the saw at a shallow angle to make the cut. Turn the saw blade vertically as you cut.

5

Drill the Handle Holes. Clamp the wood, with a piece of scrap wood underneath, to the bench. Drill the 1" (2.5cm) handle hole in both end pieces. Don't worry if the drill bites into the scrap— that's why it's there!

6

Clean Up the Holes. Wrap a small piece of 100-grit sandpaper around a dowel, or other round object. With the wood still in the vise, sand the holes smooth of any splinters.

Building: **Tool Tote**

7

Sand the Ends. Place the ends in the vise, making sure the angle cuts are level. With both hands, push the sanding block with 100-grit sandpaper back and forth on the sawn surface until the wood is smooth.

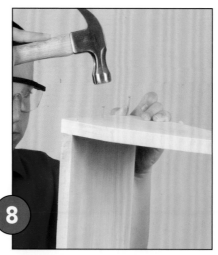

8

Join the Bottom and One End. Draw a nailing line and drive three nails (page 29) partially into one end piece. Then, drive one nail in completely. Make sure everything is lined up before you drive the other nails. If anything did shift, gently work it back into place.

9

Join the Other End. Put the tote bottom on the worktable. Stand the second end against it to make a nailing line. Start three nails and then stand the assembly upright and drive the nails in.

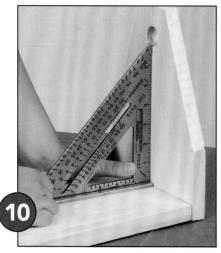

10

Square Up the Ends. Using your speed square, check whether the two end pieces are square to the tote bottom. If they're not, push them into alignment.

11

Mark the Sides. Hold one end of each side panel flush against the end piece. Mark the length by drawing along the other end piece.

12

Crosscut the Sides. Use the miter box to crosscut both side pieces the same length.

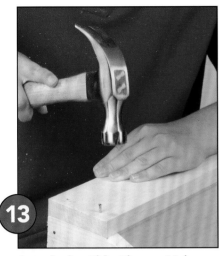

13

Attach the Side Pieces. Make nailing lines for two nails in each end of the side panels. Start the nails. Then, position the side piece so it overlaps the bottom panel. Nail it to the end pieces.

14

Nail Sides to the Bottom. Make marks for three nails on the bottom edge of each side using a pencil or an awl. Drive the nails through the sides and into the bottom.

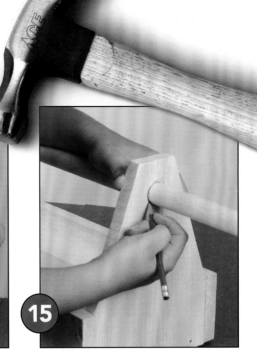

15

Cut the Dowel Handle. Fit the dowel into its holes, one end flush with an end piece. Mark where the dowel is flush with the other side. Place the dowel in the miter box and use your saw to crosscut it to the correct length.

16

Mount the Handle. Fit the handle into the holes. Drill a small pilot hole through the end piece and into the dowel.

17

Nail Locks It. Drive a finishing nail into the drilled end, locking the handle in place.

Drilling Strategy

To drill accurately, you'll need to use your whole body. Clamp your work to the table with a piece of scrap wood underneath. The scrap will keep you from drilling into the table. Stand with your feet apart and your knees flexed. Put the drill point on the mark and place one hand on the drill handle. Use your speed square to make sure the drill bit is vertical from the front and the side. Brace your holding hand with your forehead to keep it steady and maintain downward pressure. Then, turn the crank to drill the hole.

Bonus Project: Garden Tote

A tool tote can be any length with ends any shape you like. Try making the rounded ends, as shown here. Making a tote like this will introduce you to the coping saw (page 25). You'll also learn how to attach the handle with screws, instead of drilling a big hole in the end piece. To make this tote, begin by crosscutting the wood as in Steps 1 and 2 in the Tool Tote project.

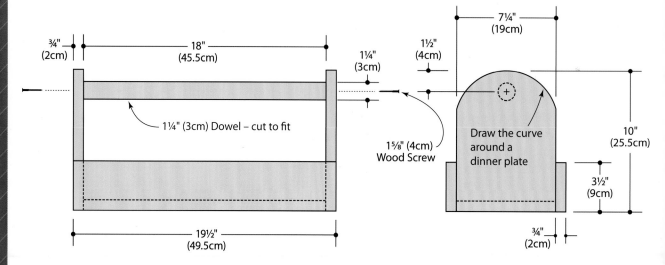

¾"
(2cm)

18"
(45.5cm)

1¼"
(3cm)

1¼" (3cm) Dowel – cut to fit

19½"
(49.5cm)

1⅝" (4cm)
Wood Screw

1½"
(4cm)

7¼"
(19cm)

Draw the curve
around a
dinner plate

10"
(25.5cm)

3½"
(9cm)

¾"
(2cm)

Building: **Garden Tote**

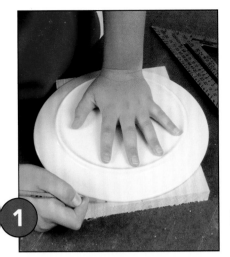

1

Lay Out the Curved Ends. Use a dinner plate as a template and draw layout lines for the rounded end pieces. Mark the holes for the handle. Then, drill them using a ⅛" (0.3cm) bit in the eggbeater drill.

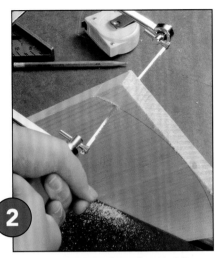

2

Saw the Curved Ends. Holding the wood upright in a vise, start at the edge of the wood and saw down to the center. Then, saw from the top down to the other side.

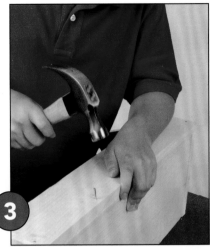

3

Assemble the Box. Nail the ends to the bottom. Make and fit the tote side panels as in Steps 7 through 14 of the Tool Tote project.

4

Make the Handle. Hold the handle dowel in place and mark its length. Remember that it fits between the two end pieces. Saw the handle to the correct length using the miter box.

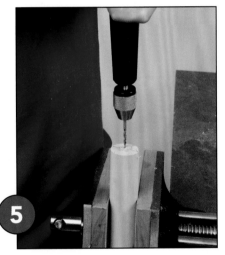

5

Drill the Handle. Using a scratch awl, make a mark in the center of each end of the dowel. Place the dowel upright in the bench vise and drill ³⁄₃₂" (0.25cm) pilot holes in both ends.

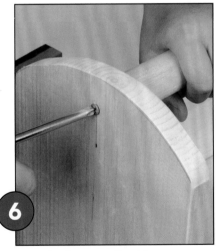

6

Attach the Handle. Use a screwdriver to start a screw through each end piece, so the point just sticks out. Fit the handle between the ends and onto the screw points. Drive both screws in.

Project: **Bluebird Nest Box**

Nest boxes provide homes for birds and are especially welcome where trees are scarce. But even if there are plenty of trees, people enjoy having nest boxes so they can watch birds build their nests and raise their young.

Your box must be sturdy, safe, and dry to protect baby birds from bad weather and predators, such as opossums, cats, and raccoons. If you build it right, predators can't open the box or reach their paws into the entrance. This nest box does not have perches, and you should not add them. That's because birds don't need them to get in and out, but predators use them to reach the baby birds. To keep the birds comfortable, you will also cut a ventilation slot at the top and add drain holes at the bottom.

The roof opens and closes with a hinge and safety catch so, at the end of the year, you can clean out the old nest and prepare your box for its next family. Wear gloves because the old nest will probably have bugs in it!

TOOLS

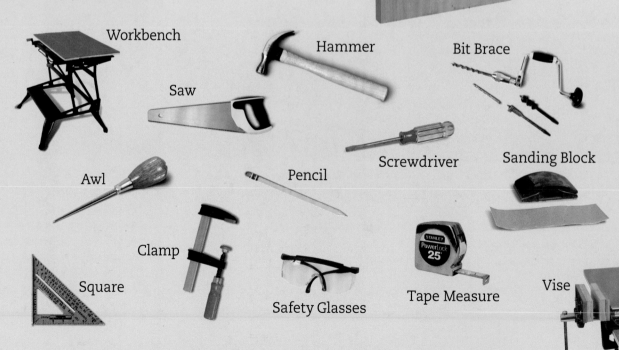

Workbench

Hammer

Bit Brace

Saw

Screwdriver

Sanding Block

Awl

Pencil

Clamp

Square

Safety Glasses

Tape Measure

Vise

Plans: **How the Nest Box Goes Together**

Nest Boxes for Other Birds

Did you know that different types of birds like different size entry holes? It seems picky but it's true! For example, the eastern bluebird prefers a hole 1⅜" (3.5cm) in diameter and 7" (18cm) to 8" (20.5cm) above the floor. They also like their nests placed about 5' (152.5cm) off the ground. The extra long back panel on this nest box lets you nail the box to a fence or tree trunk at just the right height. To customize your nest box for a different bird, research its preferences. Internet sources, local birding groups, and some fish and wildlife services may have information on your favorite bird.

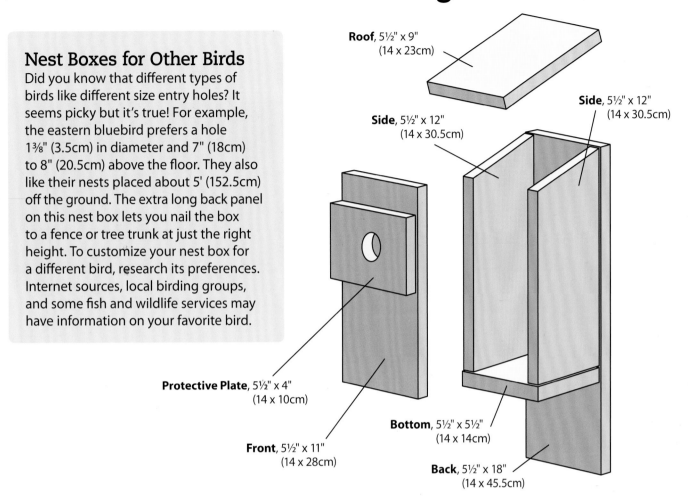

Roof, 5½" x 9" (14 x 23cm)

Side, 5½" x 12" (14 x 30.5cm)

Side, 5½" x 12" (14 x 30.5cm)

Protective Plate, 5½" x 4" (14 x 10cm)

Front, 5½" x 11" (14 x 28cm)

Bottom, 5½" x 5½" (14 x 14cm)

Back, 5½" x 18" (14 x 45.5cm)

Skills

- Measuring, page 31
- Clamping, page 24
- Crosscutting, page 34
- Drilling holes, page 27
- Sanding, page 37
- Nailing, page 29

Lumber

- 1" x 6" x 6' (2.5 x 15 x 183cm) pine or cedar

Note: Standard 1x6 pine or cedar lumber actually measures 5½" (14cm) wide by ¾" (2cm) thick.

Supplies

- 1½" (4cm) galvanized box nails, 20
- 3" (7.5cm) light strap hinge, galvanized, 1
- 2" (5cm) safety catch, galvanized, 1
- 100-grit sandpaper, 1 sheet

Sawing Layout

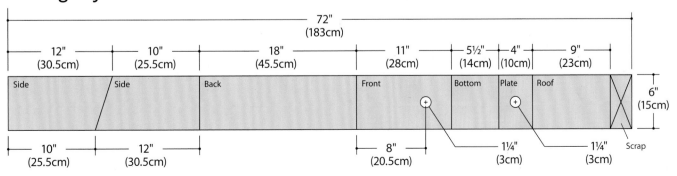

72" (183cm)

| 12" (30.5cm) | 10" (25.5cm) | 18" (45.5cm) | 11" (28cm) | 5½" (14cm) | 4" (10cm) | 9" (23cm) |

Side | Side | Back | Front | Bottom | Plate | Roof | | 6" (15cm)

10" (25.5cm) | 12" (30.5cm) | 8" (20.5cm) | 1¼" (3cm) | 1¼" (3cm) | Scrap

Building: Bluebird Nest Box

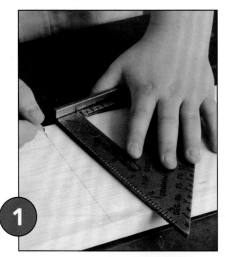

1

Draw Guidelines. Follow the sawing layout on page 61 to measure and draw layout lines across your piece of wood with a pencil. Mark the centers of the bird entry holes, too.

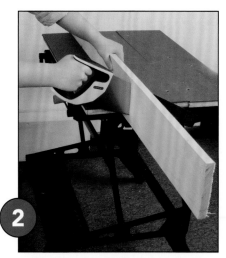

2

Crosscut the Wood. Clamp the wood to the worktable and saw the first line. Move and re-clamp after each cut. With the sanding block and 100-grit sandpaper, scrub off any splinters.

3

Drill the Bird Entry. Drill the 1⅜" (3.5cm) bird entry hole in the front panel of the nest box and in the center of the protective plate. Clamp each piece to scrap wood before drilling.

4

Nail the Doorway. Start two nails (page 29) in the doorway panel next to the entry hole. Line up the entry holes and clamp the doorway to the front panel. Hammer in both nails.

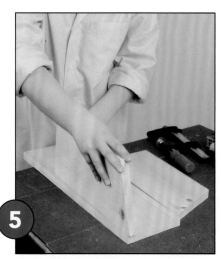

5

Lay Out the Sides. Stand each side panel on the back panel, with its point overhanging. Draw around the side panel. Use an awl or a pencil to make marks for three nails on each edge.

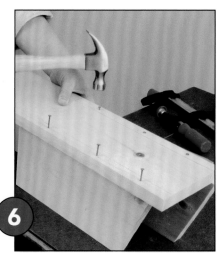

6

Lay Out the Sides. Stand each side panel on the back panel, with its point overhanging. Draw around the side panel. Use an awl or a pencil to make marks for three nails on each edge.

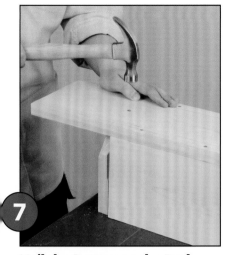

Nail the Bottom to the Back. Position the bottom panel against the back and side panels. Make a line and hammer two nails through the back into the bottom.

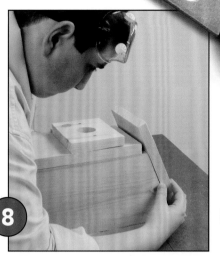

Fit the Front Panels to the Side Panels. Place the box front on the sides with the entry hole toward the top. Hold the roof in place and press the front against it. Then mark where it goes with a pencil or awl.

Nail the Front Panels to the Side Panels. Drive the first nail to fasten the front assembly to the side and bottom panels. Check that the wood hasn't moved. Then, drive two or three nails in each joint. If panels shifted, lightly tap them back into alignment.

Locate the Hinge. With the box upright, set the roof flush with the box sides and overhanging in front and back. Mark layout lines for the strap hinge on the back and roof of the box with a pencil.

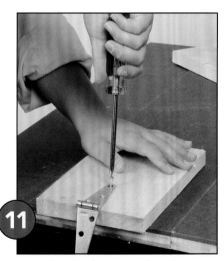

Attach Hinge to Roof and Box. Use the awl to make starter holes for the hinge screws. Screw the hinge onto the roof. Fit the roof onto the nest box and screw the hinge to the box.

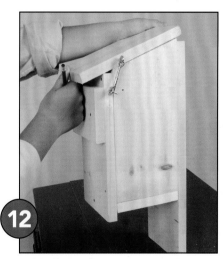

Add the Safety Catch. Drill a ⅛" (0.3cm) pilot hole and screw the safety catch to the edge of the lid. Position it near the front to keep predators out. Put the eye on the catch to place it. Then, screw the eye into the side panel.

Project: Wishbone Racer

The wishbone racer is easy to build, but the challenge is to make it go really fast. How fast yours goes will depend on how much attention you pay to the wooden wheels and axles (see Steps 3 to 10 and Speedy Wheels on page 67).

You can buy plastic or wooden wheels for toy vehicles or use wheels from old toys, but it is much more fun to build your own. Customize your wishbone racer with a cab, engines, or anything else to make it look cool. Once you understand the basics, you can build a whole fleet of vehicles: trucks, cars, trains, and airplanes.

TOOLS

Workbench

Rasp

Coping Saw

Bit Brace

Pencil

Auger Bit

Awl

Rubber Gloves

Miter Box

Paintbrush

Sanding Block

Square

Safety Glasses

Eggbeater Drill

STANLEY PowerLock 25'

Vise

Drill Bits

Tape Measure

WOODWORKING **Projects**

Plans: **How the Wishbone Racer Goes Together**

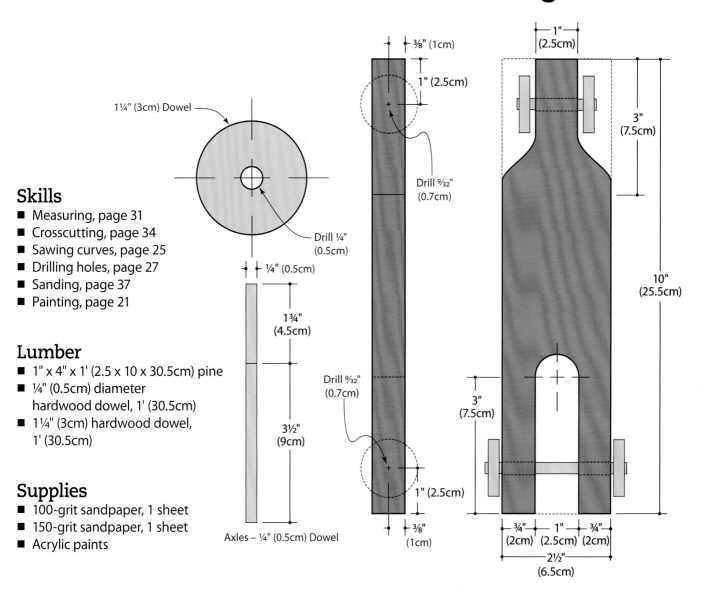

1¼" (3cm) Dowel

Drill ¼" (0.5cm)

⅜" (1cm)

1" (2.5cm)

Drill 9/32" (0.7cm)

¼" (0.5cm)

1¾" (4.5cm)

3½" (9cm)

Drill 9/32" (0.7cm)

1" (2.5cm)

⅜" (1cm)

Axles – ¼" (0.5cm) Dowel

1" (2.5cm)

3" (7.5cm)

10" (25.5cm)

3" (7.5cm)

¾" (2cm) 1" (2.5cm) ¾" (2cm)

2½" (6.5cm)

Skills
- Measuring, page 31
- Crosscutting, page 34
- Sawing curves, page 25
- Drilling holes, page 27
- Sanding, page 37
- Painting, page 21

Lumber
- 1" x 4" x 1' (2.5 x 10 x 30.5cm) pine
- ¼" (0.5cm) diameter hardwood dowel, 1' (30.5cm)
- 1¼" (3cm) hardwood dowel, 1' (30.5cm)

Supplies
- 100-grit sandpaper, 1 sheet
- 150-grit sandpaper, 1 sheet
- Acrylic paints

Finding Center for Drilling Axle Holes

To find the center, place the square corner on the outside of the wheel. Then, mark the two points where the corner crosses the wheel's edge. Use your pencil to connect these two points. Move the square corner to another place on the outside of the circle. Mark and connect two more points. The two lines you just drew should cross at the circle's center.

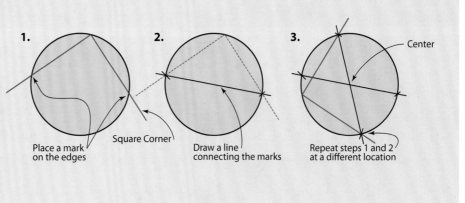

1. Place a mark on the edges — Square Corner

2. Draw a line connecting the marks

3. Repeat steps 1 and 2 at a different location — Center

Building: **Wishbone Racer**

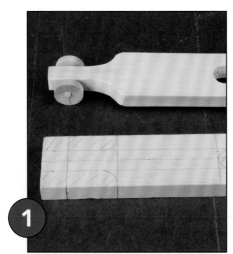

1

Lay Out the Body. Transfer the body measurements from the drawing onto a 10" (25.5cm) piece of 1x4. You can draw the curves freehand or enlarge the pattern using a copy machine and trace it.

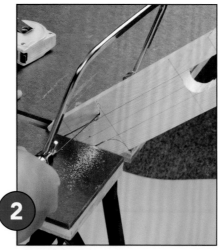

2

Saw the Body. Secure the wood in a vise and use a coping saw to cut the wishbone shape. Move it when the shape changes direction. For more on the coping saw, see page 23.

3

Locate the Axles. Mark the axle holes with your speed square. They should be 1" (2.5cm) from the ends of the car and ⅜" (1cm) from either edge.

4

Drill the Axle Holes. Drill the axle holes using the ⁹⁄₃₂" (7mm) bit in the bit brace. Slide the dowels into the holes and twirl them. They should spin freely. If they don't, ream, or widen, the holes.

5

Ream the Axle Holes. Roll a small piece of 100-grit sandpaper into a tight tube. Work it back and forth in the holes until the wheels spin freely when reattached.

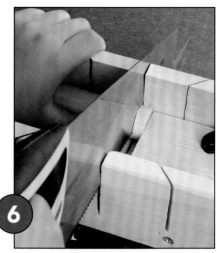

6

Make the Wheels. Place the 1¼" (3cm) dowel in the miter box. Then, measure and mark ⁵⁄₁₆" (0.8cm) from one side of the crosscut slot. Clamp a small block of wood on this mark. Push the dowel against the block and make the cuts.

Sand the Wheels. Rub each wheel on the sanding block with 100-grit sandpaper to remove splinters and round sharp corners.

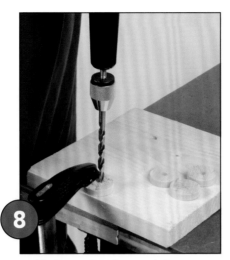

Drill the Wheels. Find the centers of the wheel blanks, as shown on the page 65, and dimple them with the scratch awl. Clamp each wheel onto a piece of scrap and drill the ¼" (0.5cm) axle hole.

Smooth the Body. Use the half-round rasp and the sanding block with 100-grit paper to smooth the body and remove sharp corners. Then, go over the entire body with 150-grit sandpaper.

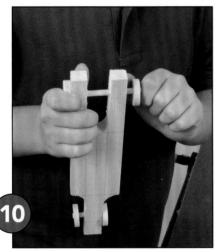

Mount the Wheels. Press a wheel on one end of each axle, insert the axles, and put wheels on the other ends. Then, take your wishbone racer for a test drive! If it doesn't roll well, go back to Step 5.

Speedy Wheels

Your racer should run on round, centered wheels and smooth-spinning axles. This photo shows two racers. The fast one on the right has a straight axle and centered wheels. The slow one on the left has a slanting axle and off-center wheels. Step 5 shows how to improve your axle holes if the wheels do not spin freely.

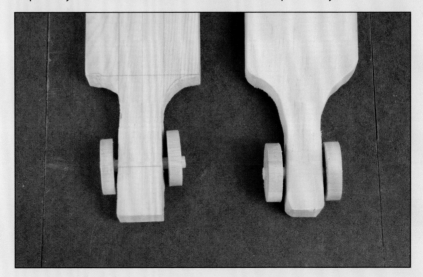

Building: **Wishbone Racer**

Paint the Car. Choose the color you want and paint the racer using the techniques on page 21. Decide on a design for your car—it can be a lightning bolt, sports team logo, or anything you want.

Prepare the Stencil. Press a piece of self-sticking kitchen shelf liner tight against the racer body with your fingers.

Cut the Design. Draw your design on the shelf liner and cut out the part you want to paint. Use the point of the knife to lift the stencil material away from the wood.

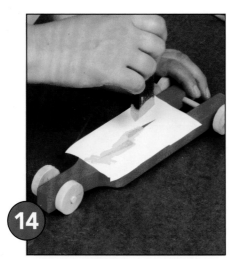

Paint the Design. Press the stencil onto the racer body and dab paint into the open part of the design. For smooth coverage, let the first coat dry for an hour. Then, apply another coat.

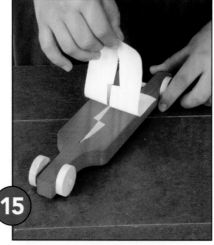

Peel the Stencil. When the paint is dry, carefully peel the stencil away from the racer body, then stand back and admire your work!

Project: Block Racer

The body of the block racer is made from a 2x4 and can be any shape you like. The wheels have spacers to keep them away from the car body. This makes the racer more stable and less likely to fall over.

This project shows you how to saw shapes in thick wood, which is more difficult than in thin wood. In addition, you'll learn how to use nails to make metal wheel axles. Metal axles make the car go even faster because they reduce the friction between the axles and the wood.

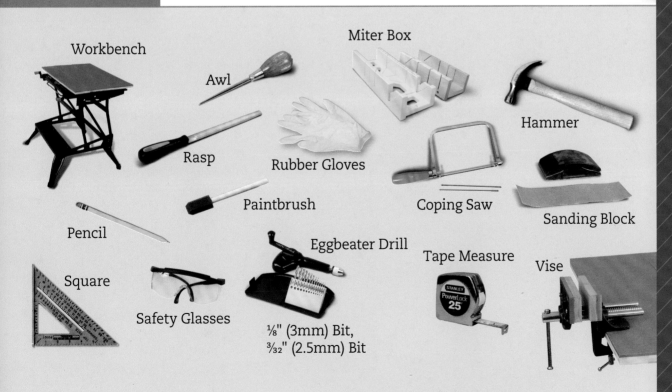

TOOLS

Workbench

Awl

Miter Box

Hammer

Rasp

Rubber Gloves

Coping Saw

Sanding Block

Paintbrush

Pencil

Eggbeater Drill

Tape Measure

Vise

Square

Safety Glasses

⅛" (3mm) Bit,
³⁄₃₂" (2.5mm) Bit

Plans: **How the Block Racer Goes Together**

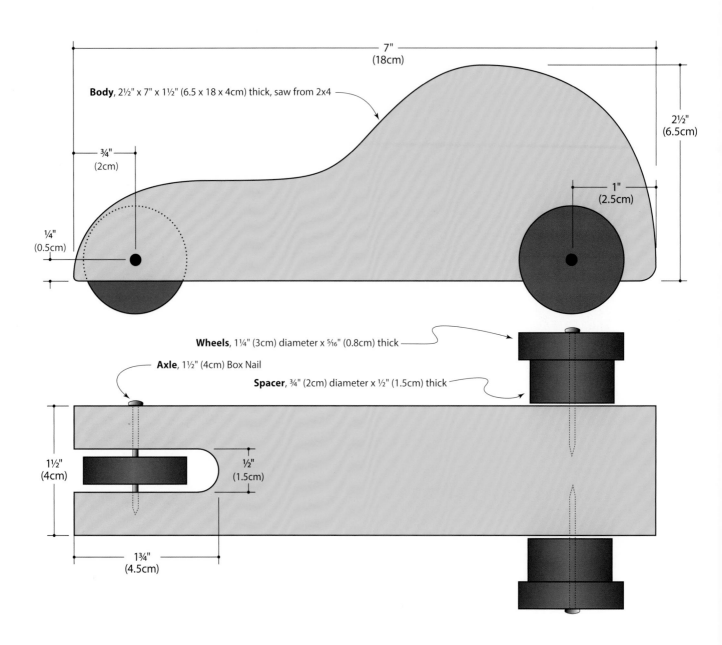

7"
(18cm)

Body, 2½" x 7" x 1½" (6.5 x 18 x 4cm) thick, saw from 2x4

2½"
(6.5cm)

¾"
(2cm)

1"
(2.5cm)

¼"
(0.5cm)

Wheels, 1¼" (3cm) diameter x ⁵⁄₁₆" (0.8cm) thick

Axle, 1½" (4cm) Box Nail

Spacer, ¾" (2cm) diameter x ½" (1.5cm) thick

1½"
(4cm)

½"
(1.5cm)

1¾"
(4.5cm)

Full-Size Pattern

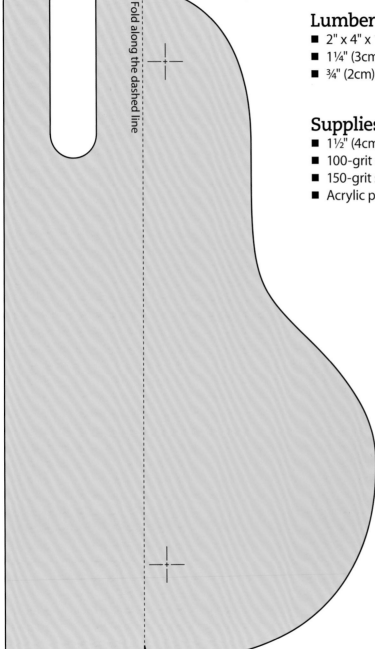

Fold along the dashed line

Skills

- Measuring, page 31
- Drilling holes, page 27
- Sawing curves, page 25
- Sanding, page 37
- Painting, page 21

Lumber

- 2" x 4" x 1' (5 x 10 x 30.5cm), fir or spruce
- 1¼" (3cm) hardwood dowel, 1' (30.5cm)
- ¾" (2cm) hardwood dowel, 1' (30.5cm)

Supplies

- 1½" (4cm) box nails, 3
- 100-grit sandpaper, 1 sheet
- 150-grit sandpaper, 1 sheet
- Acrylic paints

Sawing Shapes in Thick Wood

To help maneuver a saw in thick wood, use relief cuts. These straight cuts, made from the edge of the block to the pattern line, keep you from getting stuck in the middle of sawing a shape. In this case, once you've made the relief cuts, saw out the body and the slot for the front wheel. The wood will fall away as you pass each relief cut.

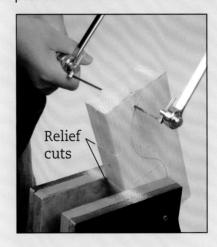

Relief cuts

Building: **Block Racer**

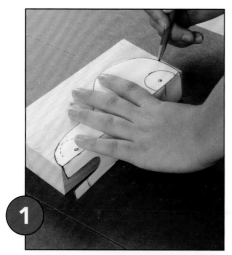

1

Lay Out the Body. Photocopy the block racer pattern. Trace its shape onto the bottom and both sides of the body blank, a 7" (18cm) block of 2x4.

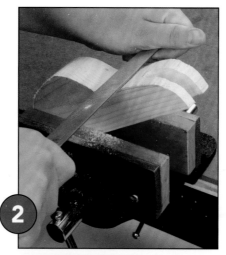

2

Saw and Smooth the Body. Saw the body in a vise (see "Sawing Shapes in Thick Wood" on page 71). Then, use a rasp and sandpaper to smooth the saw cuts and round off the sharp corners. Take your time.

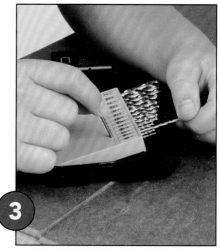

3

Drill the Axle Holes. Mark the axle holes on the racer body. Find the drill bit that is just smaller than the axle nails by testing the nails in the drill-bit case. Drill the holes.

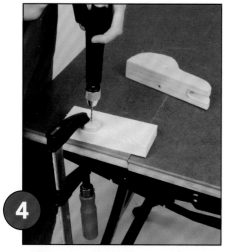

4

Make the Wheels. Use the miter box to saw the wheels. Find their centers, as shown on page 65. Drill a hole that is one size larger than the axle so the wheel spins freely.

5

Mount the Wheels. Make ½" (1.5cm)-thick dowel spacers for the rear wheels, and tap the axle nails through the wheels and into the car body. Remove the wheels to paint the racer. Reinstall them when the paint dries.

Take it for a ride and see how fast it is. You can even try racing it against the wishbone racer to see which one wins!

Bonus Project: Balloon Racer

The balloon racer moves under its own power, but it must be very light. Use either ¼" (0.5cm)-thick pieces of pine lattice molding or balsa wood from a craft store to make the body.

If you built the wishbone racer (page 64) and the block racer (page 69), you've learned most of the skills you need to make this racer. Saw all the parts according to the drawing. Glue the balloon mount onto one of the body blocks and glue the body blocks to the sides (see page 16 for gluing techniques). The wheels and axles are the same as on the block racer (page 69).

Balloon whistles are available at party shops and toy stores. The whistle reed interferes with airflow, so carefully remove it using your scratch awl. If you can't find a balloon whistle, use the barrel of a ballpoint pen. Saw off the pointed end and press the balloon nozzle into the balloon mount. Then, you'll be ready to fly!

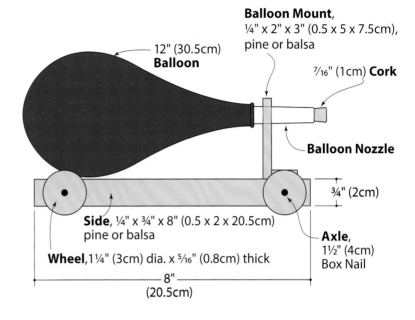

Balloon Mount, ¼" x 2" x 3" (0.5 x 5 x 7.5cm), pine or balsa

12" (30.5cm) **Balloon**

⁷⁄₁₆" (1cm) **Cork**

Balloon Nozzle

¾" (2cm)

Side, ¼" x ¾" x 8" (0.5 x 2 x 20.5cm) pine or balsa

Axle, 1½" (4cm) Box Nail

Wheel, 1¼" (3cm) dia. x ⁵⁄₁₆" (0.8cm) thick

8" (20.5cm)

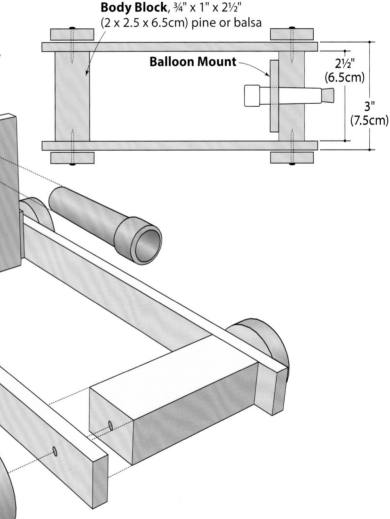

Body Block, ¾" x 1" x 2½" (2 x 2.5 x 6.5cm) pine or balsa

Balloon Mount

2½" (6.5cm)

3" (7.5cm)

Project: Keep Out Sign

For this project, you'll learn how to make wooden letters. Use the same techniques to make a welcome sign, a nameplate for your desk, or any other sign you choose. To make the message more powerful, paint the background board in one strong color and the letters in another; you might try a black background with red letters. It's up to you.

The sign shown at left uses letters cut with a coping saw from 2" (5cm) lattice molding that is ¼" (0.5cm) thick. These letters have mostly straight lines, along with drilled holes for internal curves. The full alphabet is reproduced on page 75. You can enlarge or reduce it for other projects.

TOOLS

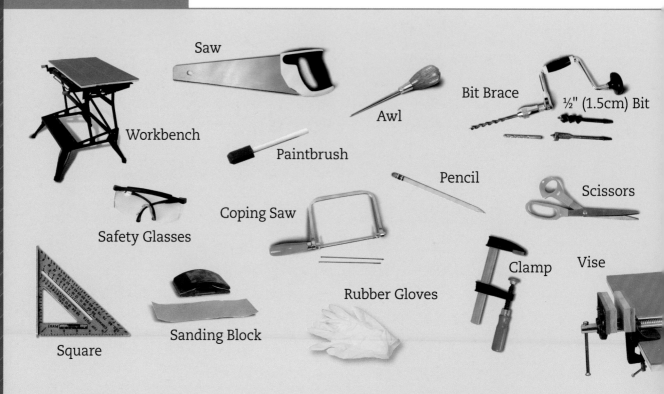

Saw

Workbench

Paintbrush

Awl

Bit Brace

½" (1.5cm) Bit

Pencil

Scissors

Safety Glasses

Coping Saw

Square

Sanding Block

Rubber Gloves

Clamp

Vise

ABCDEF
GHIJKL
MNOPQ
RSTUVW
XYZ 123
4567890

Skills
- Measuring, page 31
- Crosscutting, page 34
- Sawing curves, page 25
- Drilling holes, page 27
- Sanding, page 37
- Gluing, page 16

Lumber
- 1" x 6" x 1'
  (2.5 x 15 x 30.5cm)
  pine for sign board
- ¼" x 2" (0.5 x 5cm)
  lattice molding,
  1½" (4cm) per letter
  (12" [30.5cm] for
  Keep Out)

Supplies
- Glue stick for paper
- Wood glue
- 100-grit sandpaper,
  1 sheet
- 150-grit sandpaper,
  1 sheet
- Acrylic paints

Building: **Keep Out Sign**

Make a Paper Pattern. Use a copy machine to enlarge the alphabet to the size you want, in this project, 2" (5cm) high. Make several copies, so you can cut out all the letters your message needs.

Lay Out the Letters. Place the paper letters the thickness of a saw cut apart on the 2" (5cm) lattice molding, and glue them down with a glue stick. Tight spacing avoids a lot of sawing.

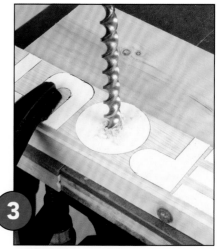

Drill the Holes. Clamp the lattice molding onto a piece of scrap wood. Use a ½" (1.5cm) bit to drill out the centers of the round letters. Drill the bowl of the U in the same way.

Sawing Shapes

After sawing the letters apart, use the coping saw to make the shapes. Clamp the letter in the bench vise, with as little as possible sticking up. Saw what you can reach, then loosen the vise and move the letter before sawing some more. Turn the letter so you are mostly sawing straight down. Saw with short, gentle strokes. If you break a letter, glue it back together and set it aside to dry before continuing to saw.

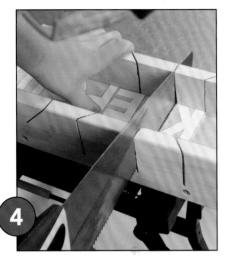

Saw the Letters Apart. Use the miter box and your hand saw to cut all the letters apart. Start sawing at the far edge of the wood, then lower the saw handle to complete the cut.

Peel the Pattern Off. Cut out all the letters using the coping saw (Sawing Shapes, left). Peel as much of the paper pattern as you can off the face of each letter.

Sand the Letter Faces. Rub the face of each letter on the sanding block to remove the rest of the pattern paper and make the wood smooth and clean.

Sand the Letter Edges. Smooth out the sawn edges of the letters with 100-grit sandpaper on the sanding block. You can hold the letter in the vise to sand it. Some letters are easiest to sand if you hold the block still and move the letter on it.

Arrange the Letters. Place the letters on the signboard and adjust the spacing so it looks good to you, then crosscut the board to length. Brush glue on each letter and clamp it in place using a spring clamp.

Paint the Sign. To make the letters stand out, paint their faces using a foam brush. Work most of the paint out of the brush before you paint, so it doesn't drip and run.

Project: Rubber Band Shooter

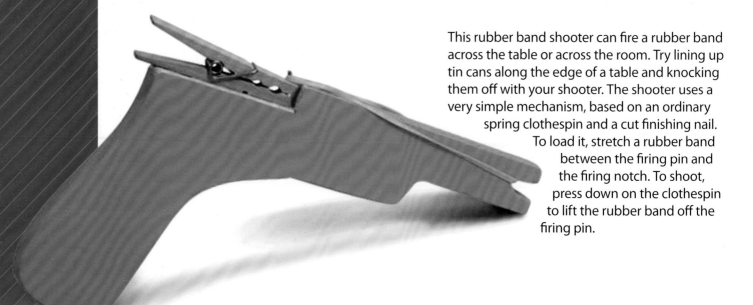

This rubber band shooter can fire a rubber band across the table or across the room. Try lining up tin cans along the edge of a table and knocking them off with your shooter. The shooter uses a very simple mechanism, based on an ordinary spring clothespin and a cut finishing nail. To load it, stretch a rubber band between the firing pin and the firing notch. To shoot, press down on the clothespin to lift the rubber band off the firing pin.

TOOLS

Saw

Paintbrush

Workbench

Pencil

Awl

Wire Cutter

Coping Saw

Eggbeater Drill

Safety Glasses

⅛" (3mm) Drill Bit

Rubber Gloves

Hammer

Tape Measure

Vise

Sanding Block

Square

Plans: **How the Shooter Goes Together**

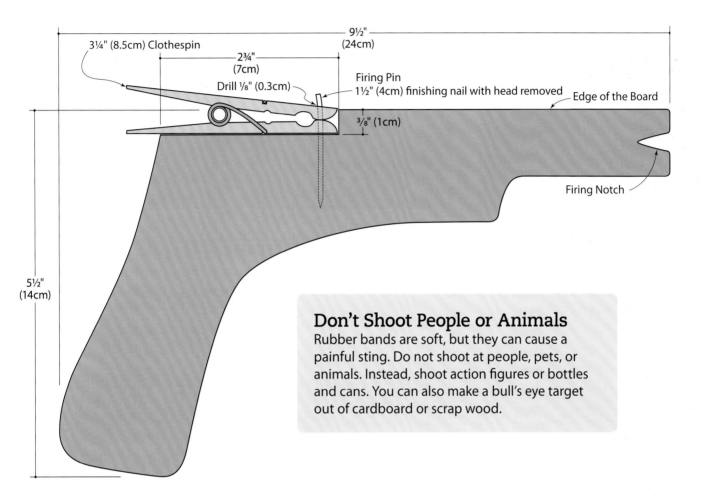

3¼" (8.5cm) Clothespin

2¾" (7cm)

9½" (24cm)

Drill ⅛" (0.3cm)

Firing Pin
1½" (4cm) finishing nail with head removed

Edge of the Board

⅜" (1cm)

Firing Notch

5½" (14cm)

Don't Shoot People or Animals
Rubber bands are soft, but they can cause a painful sting. Do not shoot at people, pets, or animals. Instead, shoot action figures or bottles and cans. You can also make a bull's eye target out of cardboard or scrap wood.

Skills
- Measuring, page 31
- Sawing shapes, page 25
- Gluing, page 16
- Drilling small holes, page 27
- Sanding, page 37

Lumber
- 1" x 6" x 1' (2.5 x 15 x 30.5cm) pine

Supplies
- 1½" (4cm) finishing nail, 1
- Wooden clothespin, 1
- Assorted rubber bands, many

Building: **Rubber Band Shooter**

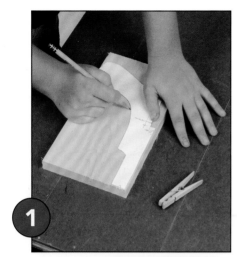

1

Transfer the Pattern. Enlarge the pattern on a photocopier. Cut it out with scissors and tape it to the wood. Place the top of the barrel flush with one edge of the wood. Trace around the pattern.

2

Lay Out the Notch. Use the speed square to check the long notch. It must be ⅜" (1cm) deep and about 2½" (6.5cm) long. Pay close attention now because this is the most critical part of the layout.

3

Saw the Long Notch. Secure the wood in a vise and use the hand saw to cut the long notch. Cut the ⅜" (1cm) side first, and then saw down to meet the first cut.

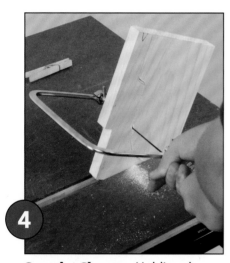

4

Saw the Shooter. Holding the wood in the vise, use a coping saw to carefully cut the body. Keep your saw square to the surface of the wood.

5

Saw the Firing Notch. Use the coping saw to cut a small V-shaped notch in the end of the shooter's barrel. One end of the rubber band is anchored here.

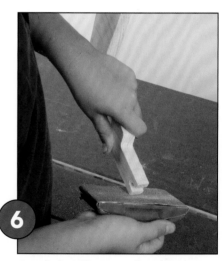

6

Sand the Shooter. Sand any sharp corners and sawing bumps off the shooter using 100-grit sandpaper on the sanding block. Sand the long notch flat and smooth.

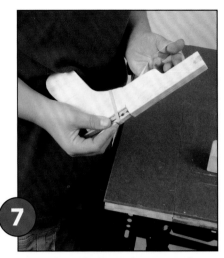

7

Glue the Clothespin. Spread wood glue on one side of the clothespin and press it into the long notch. Use a clamp or wrap the shooter with rubber bands until the glue sets.

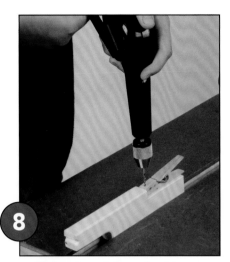

8

Drill for the Firing Pin. Use an awl to start the hole to keep the drill from wandering. Then, drill a ⅛" (0.3cm) hole through the jaws of the clothespin and into the shooter body.

9

Install the Firing Pin. Tap the firing pin into the hole, leaving about ¼" (0.5cm) inch sticking up. Test the action to be sure the clothespin trigger works smoothly. Bend the nail as needed.

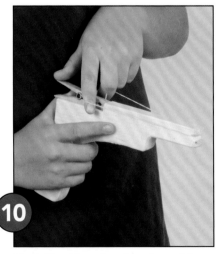

10

Test the Shooter. Hook a rubber band on the firing notch. Stretch it over the firing pin. Press down on the clothespin and away it goes!

Cutting Nails
Make the firing pin by using wire-cutting pliers to cut the head off a 1½" (4cm) finishing nail. Squeeze hard to make the cut. Make sure you and anyone around you are wearing safety goggles, since the head will go flying after you cut it. Sand the cut end of the nail smooth using 100-grit sandpaper, so there are no sharp burrs.

Project: Pop Gun

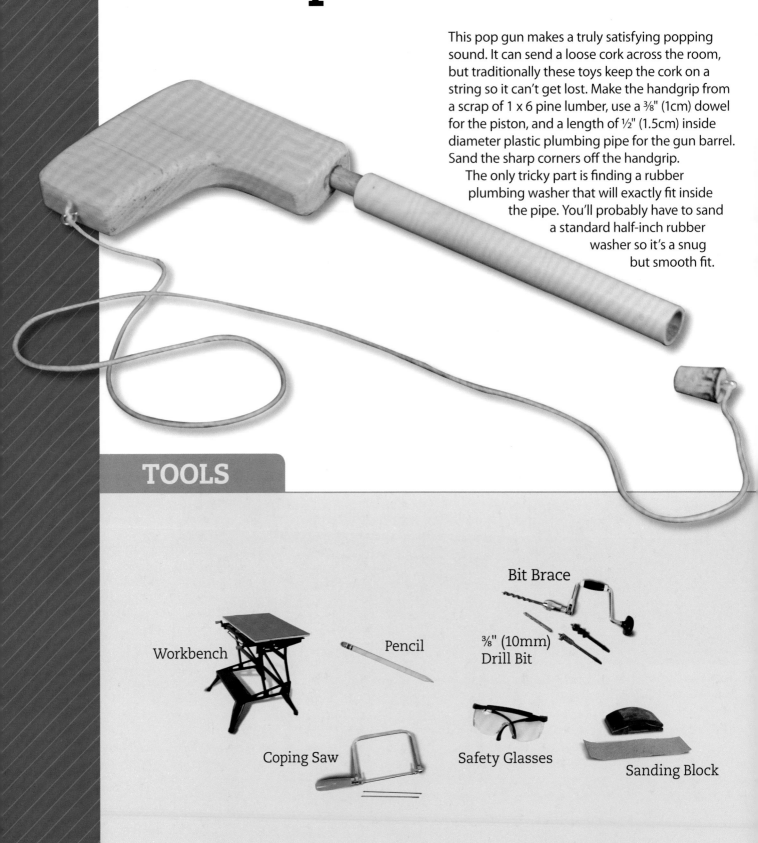

This pop gun makes a truly satisfying popping sound. It can send a loose cork across the room, but traditionally these toys keep the cork on a string so it can't get lost. Make the handgrip from a scrap of 1 x 6 pine lumber, use a ⅜" (1cm) dowel for the piston, and a length of ½" (1.5cm) inside diameter plastic plumbing pipe for the gun barrel. Sand the sharp corners off the handgrip.

The only tricky part is finding a rubber plumbing washer that will exactly fit inside the pipe. You'll probably have to sand a standard half-inch rubber washer so it's a snug but smooth fit.

TOOLS

Workbench

Pencil

Bit Brace

⅜" (10mm) Drill Bit

Coping Saw

Safety Glasses

Sanding Block

Plans: **How the Pop Gun Goes Together**

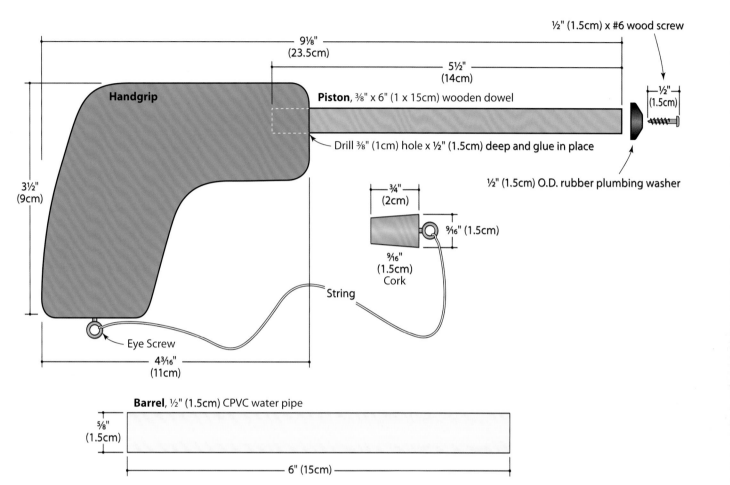

½" (1.5cm) x #6 wood screw

9⅛" (23.5cm)

5½" (14cm)

½" (1.5cm)

Handgrip

Piston, ⅜" x 6" (1 x 15cm) wooden dowel

Drill ⅜" (1cm) hole x ½" (1.5cm) deep and glue in place

½" (1.5cm) O.D. rubber plumbing washer

3½" (9cm)

¾" (2cm)

9⁄16" (1.5cm)

9⁄16" (1.5cm) Cork

String

Eye Screw

4³⁄16" (11cm)

Barrel, ½" (1.5cm) CPVC water pipe

⅝" (1.5cm)

6" (15cm)

Skills
- Sawing, page 39
- Drilling, page 27
- Sanding, page 37

Lumber
- 1" x 6" x 6" (2.5 x 15 x 15cm) pine
- ⅜" x 6" (1 x 15cm) dowel

Supplies
- ½" (1.5cm) I.D. x 6" (15cm) plastic pipe
- ½" (1.5cm) OD rubber plumbing washer
- Glue
- 2 small eye screws
- 36" (91.5cm) string
- 9⁄16" (1.5cm) cork
- ½" (1.5cm) x #6 round head screw with small washer
- 100-grit sandpaper
- Acrylic paint

Project: Adjustable Stilts

Stilts are tons of fun, and once you gain some skill walking on them, you can adjust the height to make yourself a lot taller. Practice outdoors on soft grass. These make a great gift for children who aren't too young.

Make the foot rests first; some folks call these "pegs." Glue and screw the plywood plates to the 2x4 blocks, then drill the bolt hole through both plates together.

The posts can be 5' (152.5cm) or 6' (183cm) tall, depending on your own height. Sand the wood thoroughly so you don't get splinters.

Use the completed foot rest as a jig for drilling the holes in the stilt posts.

TOOLS

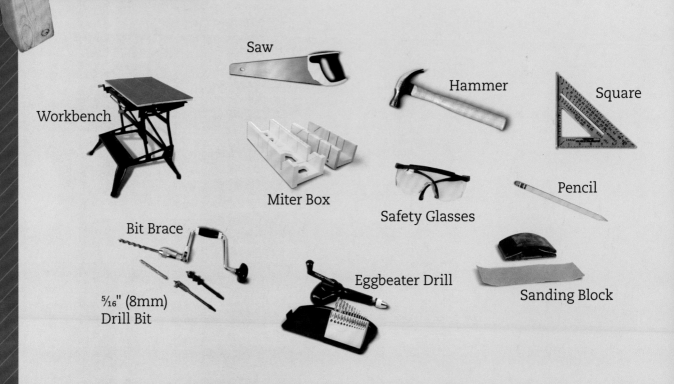

Saw

Hammer

Square

Workbench

Miter Box

Safety Glasses

Pencil

Bit Brace

Eggbeater Drill

Sanding Block

5/16" (8mm) Drill Bit

Plans: **How the Stilts Go Together**

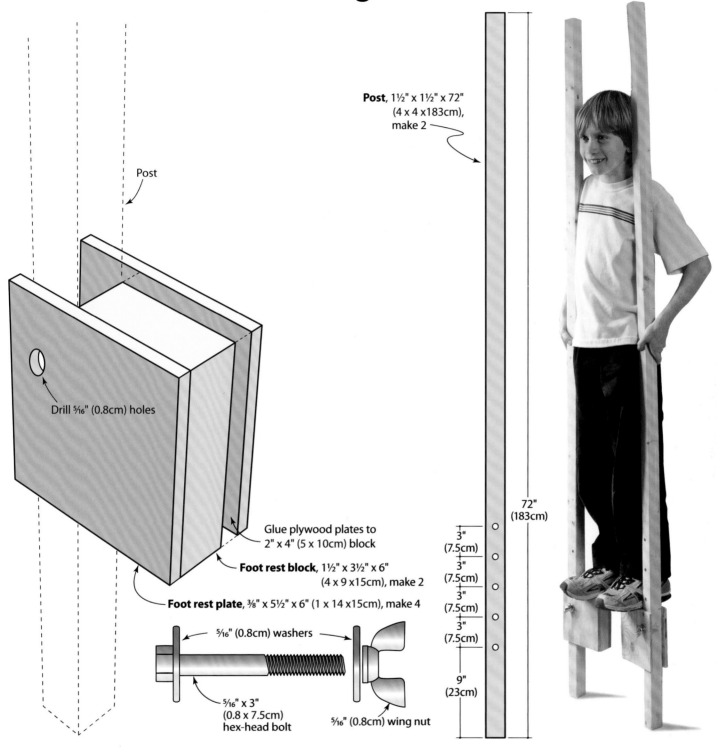

Post

Drill ⁵⁄₁₆" (0.8cm) holes

Glue plywood plates to
2" x 4" (5 x 10cm) block

Foot rest block, 1½" x 3½" x 6"
(4 x 9 x15cm), make 2

Foot rest plate, ⅜" x 5½" x 6" (1 x 14 x15cm), make 4

⁵⁄₁₆" (0.8cm) washers

⁵⁄₁₆" x 3"
(0.8 x 7.5cm)
hex-head bolt

⁵⁄₁₆" (0.8cm) wing nut

Post, 1½" x 1½" x 72"
(4 x 4 x183cm),
make 2

72"
(183cm)

3"
(7.5cm)

3"
(7.5cm)

3"
(7.5cm)

3"
(7.5cm)

9"
(23cm)

Skills

- Measuring, page 31
- Sawing, page 39
- Drilling, page 27
- Sanding, page 37

Lumber

- 2" x 2" x 72" (5 x 5 x 183cm) pine or fir
- 2" x 4" x 12" (5 x 10 x 30.5cm) pine or fir
- ⅜" x 12" x 12" (1 x 30.5 x 30.5cm) plywood

Supplies

- Two ⁵⁄₁₆" x 3" (0.8 x 7.5cm) hex-head bolts with wing nuts and extra washers
- Glue
- 1⅝" (4cm) x #8 screws
- 100-grit sandpaper

Bonus Project: Big-Foot Clompers

Clompers make a lot of noise when you stomp around inside the house. These clompers also have interchangeable footprints for making tracks in soft ground outdoors.

They are easy to make because when you glue up the blocks, you can leave a space for the rope. Knot and trim the rope so the length is comfortable for you. These make a great gift for kids!

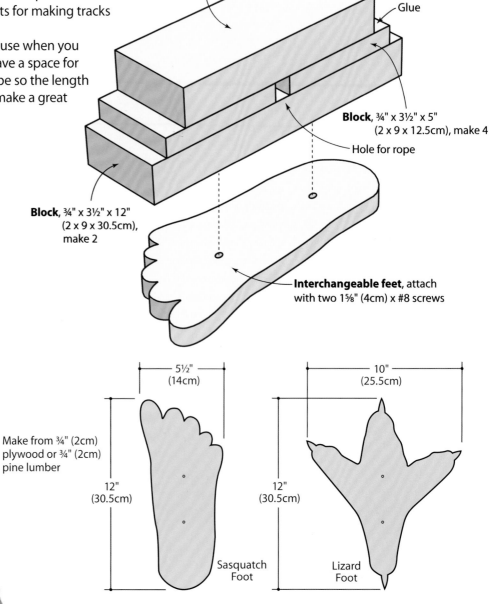

Block, 1½" x 3½" x 9" (4 x 9 x 23cm), make 2

Glue

Block, ¾" x 3½" x 5" (2 x 9 x 12.5cm), make 4

Hole for rope

Block, ¾" x 3½" x 12" (2 x 9 x 30.5cm), make 2

Interchangeable feet, attach with two 1⅝" (4cm) x #8 screws

5½" (14cm)

10" (25.5cm)

Make from ¾" (2cm) plywood or ¾" (2cm) pine lumber

12" (30.5cm)

12" (30.5cm)

Sasquatch Foot

Lizard Foot

Lumber

- 2" x 4" x 42" (5 x 10 x 106.5cm) pine or fir, blocks
- 1" x 4" x 24" (2.5 x 10 x 61cm) pine, center blocks
- ¾" x 12" x 24" (2 x 30.5 x 61cm), plywood feet
- ⁵⁄₁₆" x 12' (0.8 x 366cm), braided rope

Supplies

- Glue
- 1⅝" (4cm) x #8 screws, four
- 100-grit sandpaper

Project: Picture Frame

We'll make a picture frame and size it to hold an award certificate, a photograph, or a piece of artwork. It can have picture glass in it or not, and it can be painted or varnished, or not. If you have been learning how to carve, you could also decorate the frame with a carving motif.

The frame is held together with half-lap joints. Woodworkers usually saw and fit these joints, but that's beyond our tools so we will assemble the joints by overlapping and gluing ¼" (0.5cm) lattice molding onto the frame pieces. The key is having thin wood for the back pieces that is ½" (1.5cm) or ¾" (2cm) narrower than the main frame pieces. The frame shown uses 1x3 pine (2½" [6.5cm] wide) for the frame and ¼" (0.5cm) by 2" (5cm) lattice molding.

The difference in width of the frame and back pieces forms a ledge called a "rebate" for

mounting the artwork. Professional picture framers use this same method. They hold the artwork in place with small nails, but you can use masking tape or packing tape instead.

To build this frame you'll need to make precise measurements and crosscuts, using the miter box, and you'll need to glue and clamp carefully. Once you learn how to build this frame for an 8" (20.5cm) by 10" (25.5cm) picture, you can make one any size you like.

TOOLS

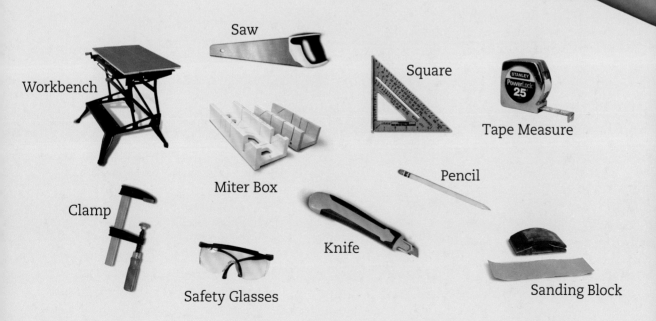

Workbench

Saw

Square

Tape Measure

Miter Box

Pencil

Clamp

Knife

Safety Glasses

Sanding Block

Plans: **How the Picture Frame Goes Together**

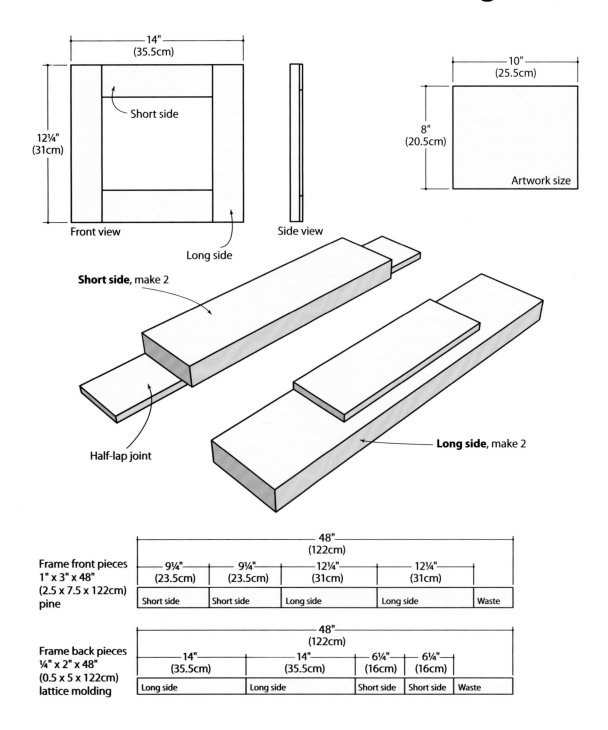

14"
(35.5cm)

12¼"
(31cm)

Short side

Front view

Long side

Side view

10"
(25.5cm)

8"
(20.5cm)

Artwork size

Short side, make 2

Half-lap joint

Long side, make 2

Frame front pieces
1" x 3" x 48"
(2.5 x 7.5 x 122cm)
pine

48" (122cm)				
9¼" (23.5cm)	9¼" (23.5cm)	12¼" (31cm)	12¼" (31cm)	
Short side	Short side	Long side	Long side	Waste

Frame back pieces
¼" x 2" x 48"
(0.5 x 5 x 122cm)
lattice molding

48" (122cm)				
14" (35.5cm)	14" (35.5cm)	6¼" (16cm)	6¼" (16cm)	
Long side	Long side	Short side	Short side	Waste

Skills
- Measuring, page 31
- Crosscutting, page 34
- Gluing, page 16
- Sanding, page 37

Lumber
- 1" x 3" x 48" (2.5 x 7.5 x 122cm) pine
- ¼" x 2" x 48" (0.5 x 5 x 122cm) pine lattice molding

Supplies
- Woodworking glue
- 100-grit sandpaper
- 150-grit sandpaper

Building: **Picture Frame**

1

Measure and Crosscut the Frame Piece. Measure and crosscut two short frame pieces, two long frame pieces, two long back pieces, and two short back pieces. Use the miter box and work carefully.

2

Position the Short Frame Pieces. Center the short frame pieces on top of the long back pieces. The frame piece and the back piece should be flush on one long edge. Mark the pieces.

3

Glue the First Pair. Brush glue onto the back side of both short frame pieces, and on the front side of both long back pieces. Position each pair of pieces as in Step 2.

Proper Measurements

For 8" x 10" (20.5 x 25.5cm) artwork, follow the measurements given in the Sawing Layout. For other sizes, measure the long dimension of the artwork and subtract ¾" (2cm); that's the length of the short frame pieces. Measure the short dimension of the artwork and add 4¼" (11cm) ; that's the length of the long frame pieces. The long back pieces, which hold the frame together, are 6" (15cm) longer than the short frame pieces. The two short back pieces are cut to fit in Step 2, above. About ⅜" (1cm) around the edge of the artwork will be hidden by the frame.

Building: **Picture Frame**

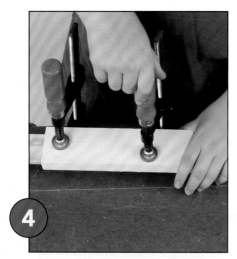

4

Clamp the Wood. Clamp the two sandwiches of short frame pieces and long back pieces to the worktable, with two clamps on each. Let it dry for an hour.

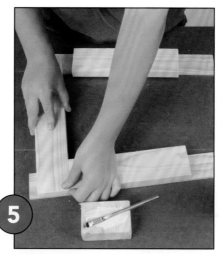

5

Fit One Long Frame Piece. Fit the two long side pieces onto the protruding back pieces. Glue and clamp one piece in place but don't wait for the glue to dry.

6

Glue the Other Long Frame Piece. Glue and clamp the other long frame piece to the assembled frame. You might have to loosen the first joint to push the frame square and tight. Let it dry an hour.

7

Fit the Last Two Back Pieces. Hold the remaining two back pieces up to the assembled frame and mark their length. Use the miter box to crosscut both pieces.

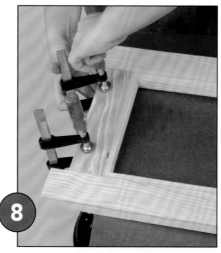

8

Glue the Back Pieces. Spread glue on the two short back pieces and press them into place. Line up their outside edges with the frame pieces, and clamp until the glue dries.

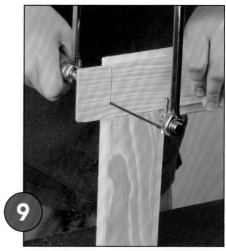

9

Trim the Long Pieces. The two long back pieces protrude at each end. Use the coping saw to cut them as close as you can to the edges of the frame. Try not to scuff the frame itself.

10

Sand the Frame Edges. Hold the picture frame edge-up in the bench vise. With 100-grit sandpaper on the sanding block, sand all four edges of the picture frame.

11

Paint the Frame. Choose a frame color that shows off your artwork, and paint both sides of the frame. Try to keep paint out of the rebate.

12

Mount the Artwork. Cut a backing piece of heavy paper or mat board the same size as the artwork. Tape the backing piece and the artwork into the frame rebate.

A Strong Joint

The glued half-lap is a strong joint that will hold your frame together. Be sure you spread glue on the flat part of the joint as well as on the end of the frame piece. Trim and sand the joint after the glue has dried.

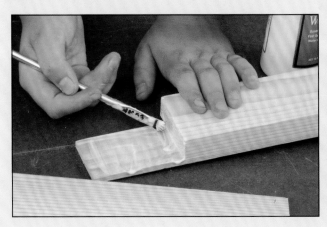

Project: **Bookcase**

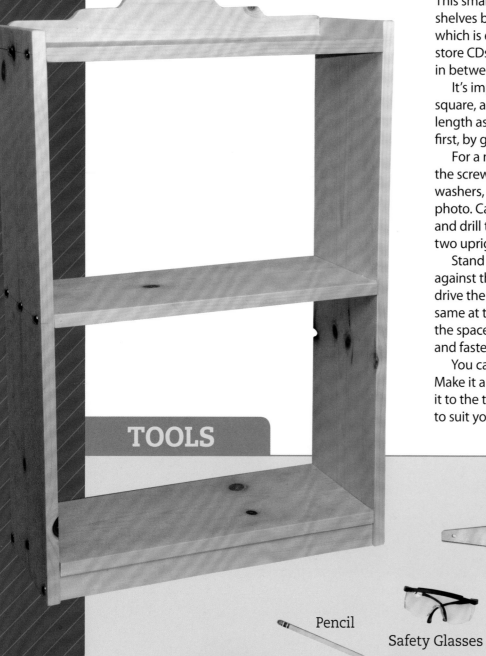

This small bookcase does not have adjustable shelves but they are spaced 13" (33cm) apart, which is enough for most books. If you want to store CDs and DVDs, add intermediate shelves in between the ones shown.

It's important that all of the shelves be sawn square, and the rail pieces be exactly the same length as the shelves. Make the base assembly first, by gluing two rails to the bottom shelf.

For a neat appearance, all of the screws go through finishing washers, as shown in the photo. Carefully measure, mark, and drill the pilot holes in the two uprights.

Stand one of the uprights against the base assembly and drive the three screws. Do the same at the other end. Now use the spacer, and a small clamp or two, to position and fasten each shelf, as shown in the photo.

You can make the top rail any shape you like. Make it a good fit between the uprights and glue it to the top shelf. Paint or varnish the bookcase to suit yourself.

TOOLS

Saw

Clamp

Pencil

Square

Safety Glasses

Workbench

Miter Box

Eggbeater Drill

Sanding Block

Plans: **How the Bookcase Goes Together**

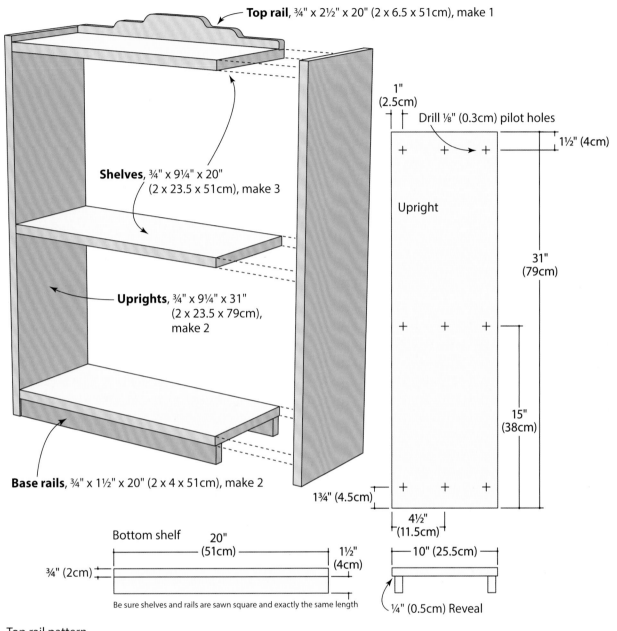

Top rail, ¾" x 2½" x 20" (2 x 6.5 x 51cm), make 1

1"
(2.5cm)

Drill ⅛" (0.3cm) pilot holes

1½" (4cm)

Upright

31"
(79cm)

Shelves, ¾" x 9¼" x 20"
(2 x 23.5 x 51cm), make 3

Uprights, ¾" x 9¼" x 31"
(2 x 23.5 x 79cm),
make 2

15"
(38cm)

1¾" (4.5cm)

4½"
(11.5cm)

Base rails, ¾" x 1½" x 20" (2 x 4 x 51cm), make 2

Bottom shelf

20"
(51cm)

1½"
(4cm)

¾" (2cm)

Be sure shelves and rails are sawn square and exactly the same length

10" (25.5cm)

¼" (0.5cm) Reveal

Top rail pattern

Each square equals 1" (2.5cm)

Skills
- Measuring, page 31
- Sawing, page 39
- Sanding, page 37
- Gluing, page 16
- Drilling, page 27
- Driving screws, page 40

Lumber
- 1" x 10" x 12' (2.5 x 25.5 x 366cm)
  No. 2 pine
- 1" x 2" x 6' (2.5 x 5 x 183cm)
  No 2. pine

Supplies
- Glue
- 100-grit sandpaper
- 2" (5cm) x #8 flathead screws, 18
- #10 finishing washers, 18

Project: Marble Roll

Marble rolls are tons of fun and this one can be rearranged in a million different ways. That's because the track sections have magnetic weather stripping glued onto the sides. You can stick them onto the refrigerator or a filing cabinet or any other large, vertical surface that's made of iron or steel.

Assemble the track sections with glue, from short lengths of cove and lattice molding. The materials listed here will make nine sections. If you are lucky, your lattice will be exactly the same width as two pieces of cove. If not, when the glue dries you'll have to sand the lattice flush with the cove, using 100-grit sandpaper on a hard rubber block.

Glue an end piece on one end of each track section, and on both ends of one-track section, the last one in the roll. That way it will catch the marbles as they come down.

TOOLS

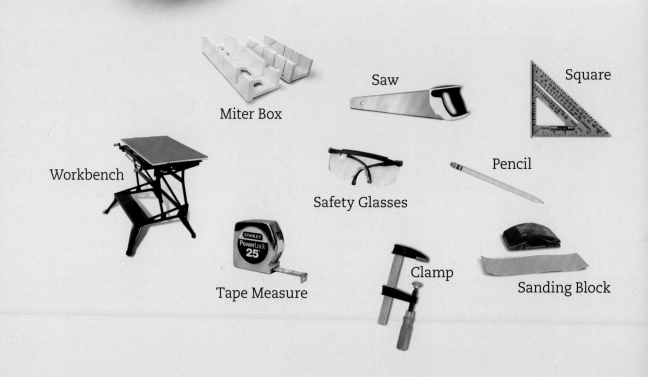

Miter Box

Saw

Square

Workbench

Safety Glasses

Pencil

Tape Measure

Clamp

Sanding Block

Plans: **How the Marble Roll Goes Together**

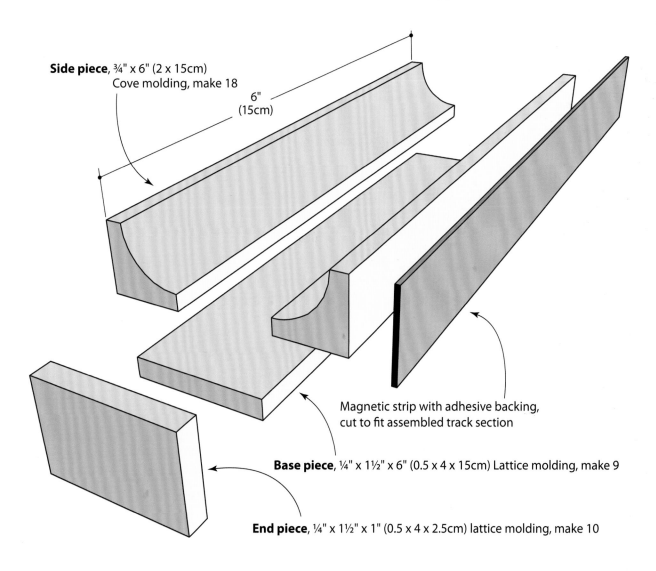

Side piece, ¾" x 6" (2 x 15cm)
Cove molding, make 18

6"
(15cm)

Magnetic strip with adhesive backing,
cut to fit assembled track section

Base piece, ¼" x 1½" x 6" (0.5 x 4 x 15cm) Lattice molding, make 9

End piece, ¼" x 1½" x 1" (0.5 x 4 x 2.5cm) lattice molding, make 10

Assembly sequence

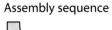

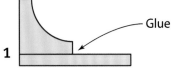 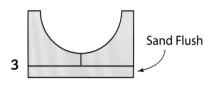

1   Glue

2   Glue

3   Sand Flush

Skills
- Measuring, page 31
- Sawing, page 39
- Sanding, page 37
- Gluing, page 16

Lumber
- ¾" x ¾" x 10' (2 x 2 x 305cm)
  cove molding, track
- ¼" x 1½" x 6' (0.5 x 4 x 183cm)
  lattice molding, track base

Supplies
- Glue
- 100-grit sandpaper
- 1" x 6' (2.5 x 183cm)
  flexible magnetic stripping
- Acrylic paint

Project: Rubber Band-Powered Paddleboat

The paddleboat propels itself, with the aid of some twisted rubber bands. Make the hull first, and then glue the side rails to it. Trim the rails to the line of the prow, then glue on the two forward rails. You can reinforce the glue joints with a few small nails.

Make the pilothouse out of any wood scrap you have on hand. Make it taller or wider to suit yourself. To fasten a smoke stack, first glue it to the roof, then drill a pilot hole from below and lock it in place with one screw.

Assemble the four paddle pieces with glue and nails, first in two pairs, then glue the pairs together. Make sure the blades follow around as shown in the drawing. Mount the paddle with at least two rubber bands, then wind it up and watch it scoot across the water.

TOOLS

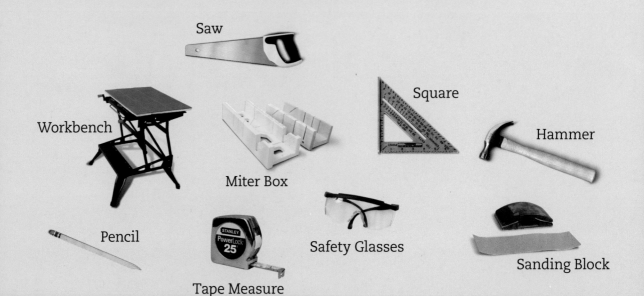

Saw

Square

Workbench

Hammer

Miter Box

Safety Glasses

Pencil

Sanding Block

Tape Measure

Plans: **How the Paddleboat Goes Together**

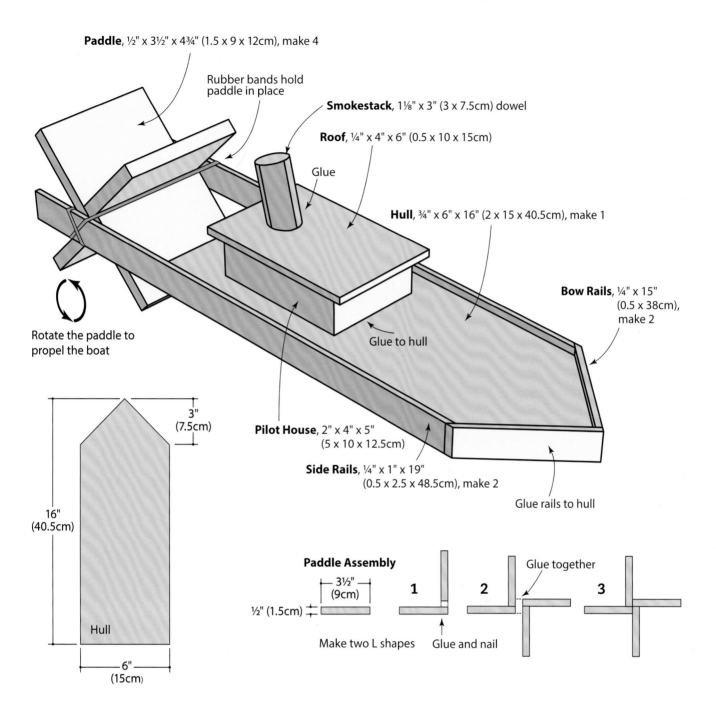

Paddle, ½" x 3½" x 4¾" (1.5 x 9 x 12cm), make 4

Rubber bands hold paddle in place

Smokestack, 1⅛" x 3" (3 x 7.5cm) dowel

Roof, ¼" x 4" x 6" (0.5 x 10 x 15cm)

Glue

Hull, ¾" x 6" x 16" (2 x 15 x 40.5cm), make 1

Glue to hull

Bow Rails, ¼" x 15" (0.5 x 38cm), make 2

Rotate the paddle to propel the boat

Pilot House, 2" x 4" x 5" (5 x 10 x 12.5cm)

Side Rails, ¼" x 1" x 19" (0.5 x 2.5 x 48.5cm), make 2

Glue rails to hull

3" (7.5cm)

16" (40.5cm)

Hull

6" (15cm)

Paddle Assembly

3½" (9cm)

½" (1.5cm)

Make two L shapes

Glue and nail

1   **2**   **3**

Glue together

Skills
- Measuring, page 31
- Sawing, page 39
- Gluing, page 16
- Nailing, page 29

Lumber
- 1" x 6" x 16" (2.5 x 15 x 40.5cm) No. 2 pine
- ¼" x 1" x 48" (0.5 x 2.5 x 122cm) Lattice Molding
- ½" x 4" x 24" (1.5 x 10 x 61cm) pine
- 2" x 4" x 5" (5 x 10 x 12.5cm) pine or fir
- ¼" x 4" x 6" (0.5 x 10 x 15cm) plywood
- 1⅛" x 3" (3 x 7.5cm) dowel

Supplies
- Waterproof wood glue or epoxy
- Small nails
- 100-grit sandpaper
- Acrylic paint

Project: Exploding Marble Target

The exploding castle wall is a terrific target for playing marbles. A strong rubber band holds the castle tower in place. When you hit the target with a marble, the force pushes the plug out of the doorway, allowing the rubber band to toss the tower into the air.

You'll be able to adapt this idea to make an exploding target look like anything you want.

TOOLS

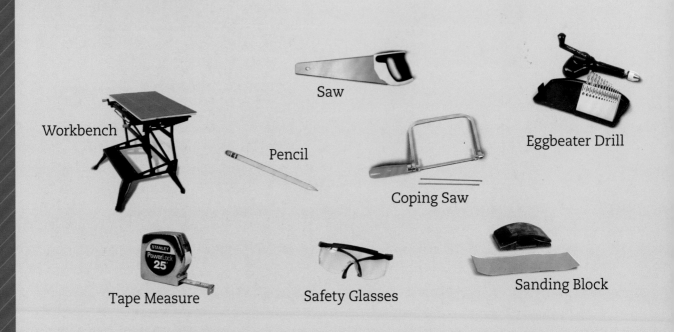

Workbench

Saw

Pencil

Coping Saw

Eggbeater Drill

Tape Measure

Safety Glasses

Sanding Block

Plans: **How the Target Goes Together**

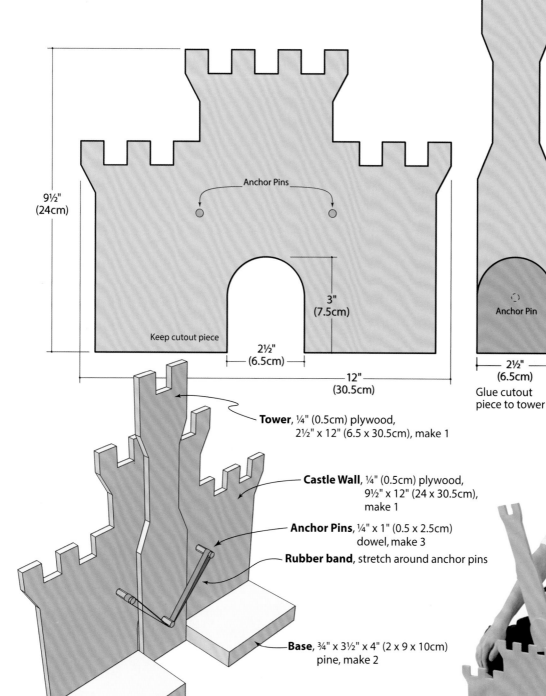

9½"
(24cm)

Anchor Pins

3"
(7.5cm)

Keep cutout piece

2½"
(6.5cm)

12"
(30.5cm)

12"
(30.5cm)

Anchor Pin

2½"
(6.5cm)

Glue cutout
piece to tower

Tower, ¼" (0.5cm) plywood,
2½" x 12" (6.5 x 30.5cm), make 1

Castle Wall, ¼" (0.5cm) plywood,
9½" x 12" (24 x 30.5cm),
make 1

Anchor Pins, ¼" x 1" (0.5 x 2.5cm)
dowel, make 3

Rubber band, stretch around anchor pins

Base, ¾" x 3½" x 4" (2 x 9 x 10cm)
pine, make 2

Skills
- Sawing, page 39
- Sanding, page 37
- Drilling, page 27
- Gluing, page 16

Lumber
- ¼" x 12" x 12" (0.5 x 30.5 x 30.5cm)
  smooth plywood
- 1" x 4" x 8" (2.5 x 10 x 20.5cm) pine
- ¼" x 6" (0.5 x 15cm) dowel

Supplies
- Glue
- 1 strong rubber band
- 100-grit sandpaper
- 4 #6 x 1" (2.5cm) flathead wood screws
- Acrylic paint

Project: Catapult

The catapult is powered by four thick rubber bands, which pack enough energy to lob a ball over the sofa. The version shown here uses a wooden kitchen spoon as the launching arm, but you could substitute any flat and thin piece of wood.

Make the frame first, joining the corners with #6 wood screws: be sure you drill pilot holes or else the wood will split. Then cut the armature uprights and make the crosspiece to fit. It should be the same length as the outside width of the assembled frame.

The anchor pins hold the ends of the four rubber bands. The locking pins keep the rubber bands from unwinding. Glue the short anchor pins into their holes in the frame sides. Thread the rubber bands into the holes, around the spoon handle, and around the locking pins. Pull the locking pins away from the frame sides to wind up the rubber band.

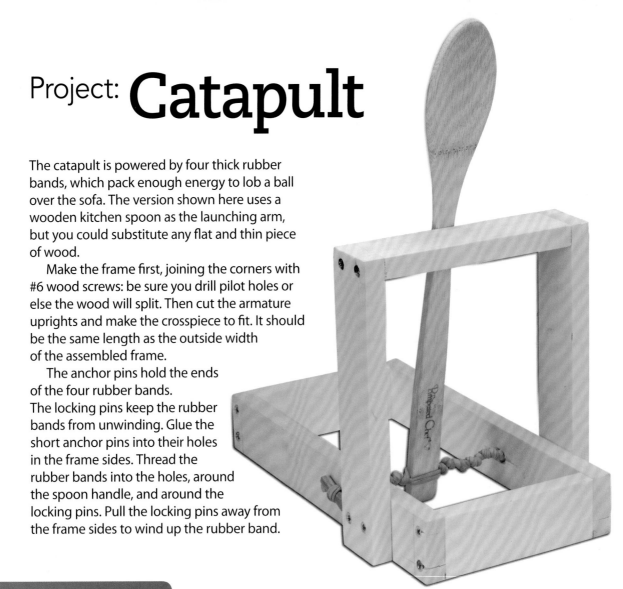

TOOLS

Workbench

Saw

Bit Brace

¼" (5mm) Drill Bit

Screwdriver

Eggbeater Drill

Miter Box

Vise

Pencil

Safety Glasses

Sanding Block

Tape Measure

Plans: **How the Catapult Goes Together**

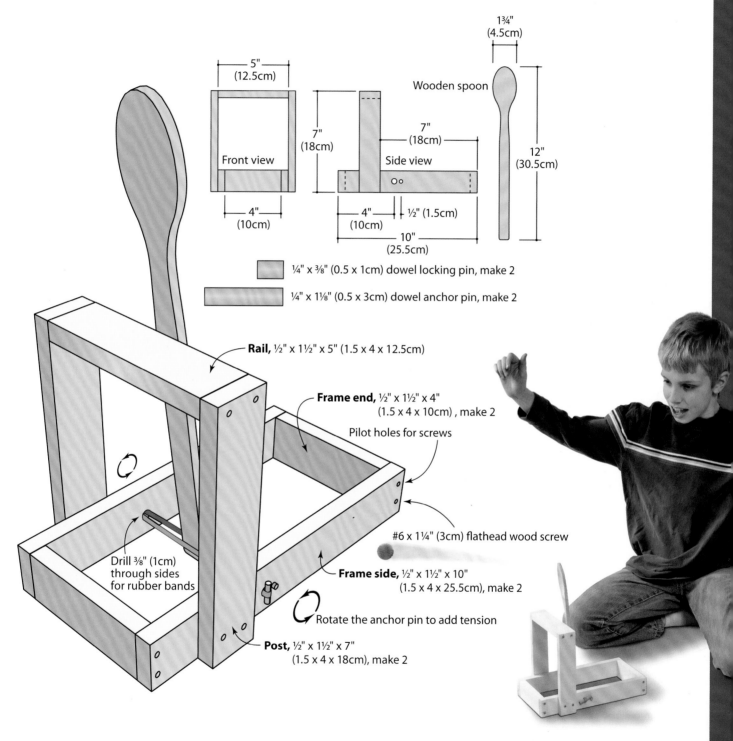

5" (12.5cm)

7" (18cm)

Front view

4" (10cm)

Side view

7" (18cm)

4" (10cm)

½" (1.5cm)

10" (25.5cm)

1¾" (4.5cm)

Wooden spoon

12" (30.5cm)

¼" x ⅜" (0.5 x 1cm) dowel locking pin, make 2

¼" x 1⅛" (0.5 x 3cm) dowel anchor pin, make 2

Rail, ½" x 1½" x 5" (1.5 x 4 x 12.5cm)

Frame end, ½" x 1½" x 4" (1.5 x 4 x 10cm) , make 2

Pilot holes for screws

#6 x 1¼" (3cm) flathead wood screw

Frame side, ½" x 1½" x 10" (1.5 x 4 x 25.5cm), make 2

Drill ⅜" (1cm) through sides for rubber bands

Rotate the anchor pin to add tension

Post, ½" x 1½" x 7" (1.5 x 4 x 18cm), make 2

Skills
- Measuring, page 31
- Sawing, page 39
- Drilling, page 27
- Driving screws, page 40
- Sanding, page 37

Lumber
- ½" x 1½" x 48" (1.5 x 4 x 122cm) pine
- ½" x 6" (1.5 x 15cm) dowel
- 12" (30.5cm) wooden spoon

Supplies
- 1¼" (3cm) x #6 flat head wood screws, 16
- 4 strong rubber bands
- 100-grit sandpaper
- Acrylic paint

Project: Wiggly Snake

The wiggly snake is a lot of fun. It's made out of 1½" (4cm) lattice molding, which is ¼" (0.5cm) thick. The head and tail segments are each different, but the middle links are all the same. You can make the snake as long as you like, and you can paint it any way you like.

Saw the molding into blanks using the miter box. Use the coping saw to shape the head and tail, and to make the cutouts. Drill the small holes for the wire links after sawing.

The only trick is bending the wire links that hold the snake together. Do it with needle-nose pliers, by cutting the wire to length, making a loop in one end of it, threading it through the snake parts, making the locking loop in its other end, and cutting off any excess.

TOOLS

Saw

Square

Coping Saw

Workbench

Pencil

Miter Box

Needle-nose Pliers

Tape Measure

Safety Glasses

Eggbeater Drill

Sanding Block

Plans: **How the Snake Goes Together**

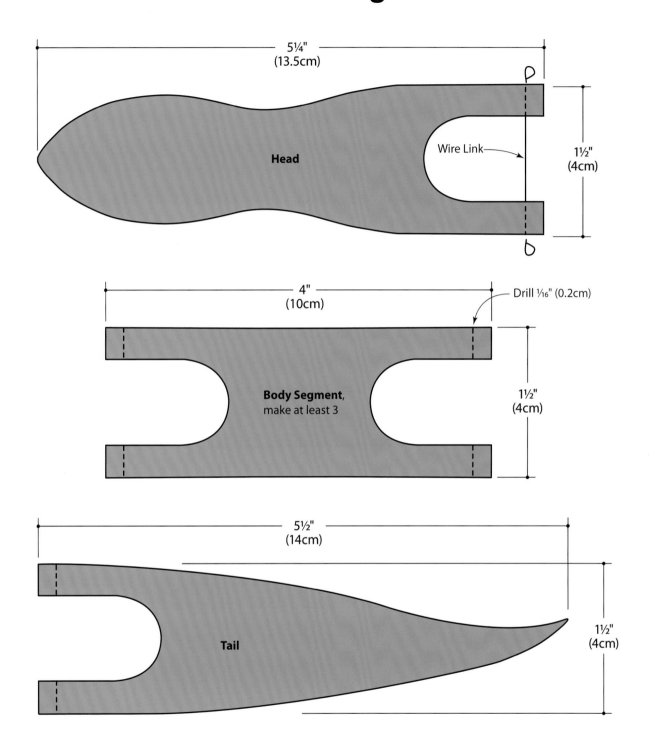

5¼"
(13.5cm)

Head

Wire Link

1½"
(4cm)

4"
(10cm)

Drill ¹⁄₁₆" (0.2cm)

Body Segment,
make at least 3

1½"
(4cm)

5½"
(14cm)

Tail

1½"
(4cm)

Skills
- Measuring, page 31
- Sawing, page 25
- Cutting wire, page 81

Lumber
- ¼" x 1½" x 24" (0.5 x 4 x 61cm) Lattice Molding

Supplies
- #20 x 24" (61cm) Craft Wire
- 100-grit Sandpaper
- Acrylic Paint

Project: Coffee Can Birdhouse

This simple birdhouse uses an old coffee can as the home for whichever birds decide to move in. Be sure to clean out all the coffee remnants before building the house!

The techniques for making this birdhouse are similar to the Bluebird Nest Box. Examine the patterns, look at the photos, and read through the tips on page 107 before beginning the project.

TOOLS

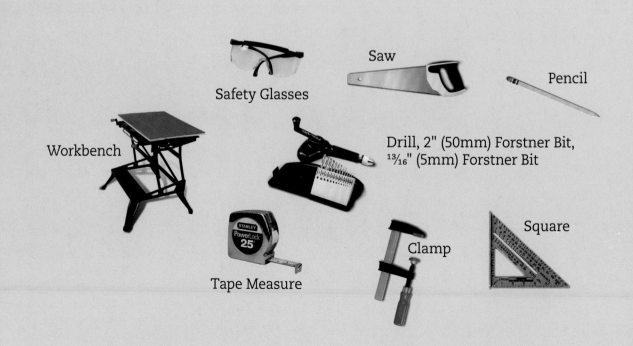

Safety Glasses

Saw

Pencil

Workbench

Drill, 2" (50mm) Forstner Bit, ¹³⁄₁₆" (5mm) Forstner Bit

Tape Measure

Clamp

Square

Plans: **How the Coffee Can Birdhouse Goes Together**

Front View

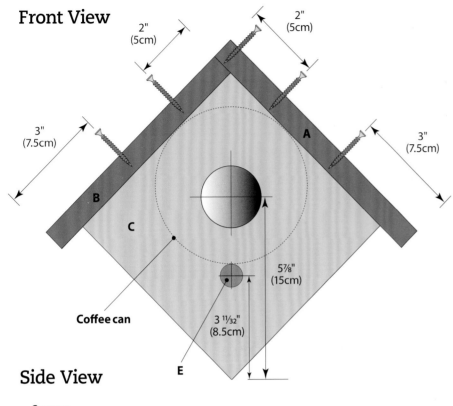

2"
(5cm)

2"
(5cm)

3"
(7.5cm)

3"
(7.5cm)

A

B

C

Coffee can

5⅞"
(15cm)

3 ¹¹/₃₂"
(8.5cm)

E

Side View

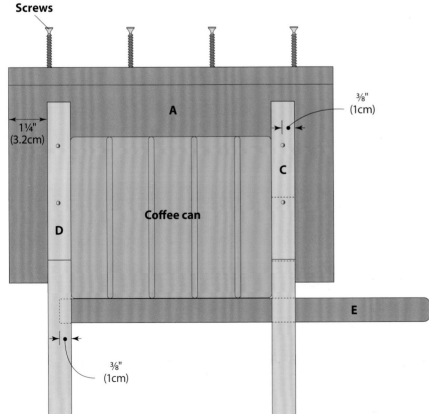

Screws

1¼"
(3.2cm)

A

C

D

Coffee can

E

⅜"
(1cm)

⅜"
(1cm)

Skills

- Painting, page 21
- Clamping, page 24
- Sawing, page 25
- Drilling, page 27
- Measuring, page 31
- Sanding, page 37
- Driving screws, page 40

Lumber/Project Pieces

- Right top (A): ¾" x 8¾" x 10½"
  (2 x 22 x 27cm) preferred wood
- Left top (B):
  ¾" x 8" x 10½" (2 x 20.5 x 27cm)
  preferred wood
- Front (C): ¾" x 7" x 7"
  (2 x 18 x 18cm) preferred wood
- Back (D): ¾" x 7" x 7"
  (2 x 18 x 18cm) preferred wood
- Perch (E): ¾" x 12"
  (2 x 30.5cm) dowel

Supplies

- 1 lb. coffee can, 5⅛"-O.D. x 6½"
  (13 x 16.5cm)
- Double-sided tape
- #6 x 1⅝" (4cm) wood screws, 12
- 1⅜" (3.5cm) screw eyes, 2
- Clothes hanging wire
- Wood glue

You can choose to decorate your birdhouse coffee can with paint, stickers, or even small tiles as pictured.

Depending on the type of wood you choose and the color of the can, you can create many different birdhouses with unique looks.

Building: Coffee Can Birdhouse

Here are some tips for building your birdhouse.

1

Hole and Perch Locations. Refer to the front view drawing for the front hole and perch's locations. Transfer these locations to the front piece and drill the front hole. Gang the front and back pieces together using double-sided tape.

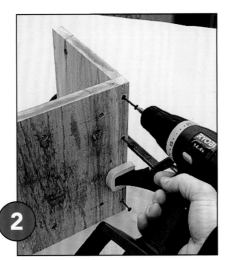

2

Fastening Roof Pieces. Clamp the two roof pieces together with the right top overhanging the left top. Use the wood screws to fasten the two together.

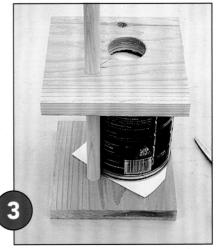

3

Proper Spacing. Assemble the front, back, and perch pieces together with the coffee can between them. Place a piece of paper between the coffee can and the front and back pieces to allow for expansion.

4

Set Up the Front and Back. Use a piece of scrap wood to raise the front and back centered with the roof.

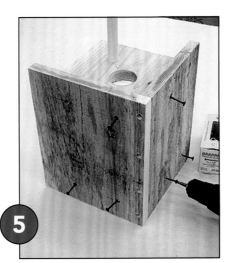

5

Fasten Front and Back. Fasten the roof to the front and back with the wood screws.

6

Attach Hanging Wire. Use the two screw eyes and the clothes wire to hang the birdhouse from a limb in a tree. Place the screw eyes a fair distance apart and on opposite roof top pieces.

Project: Butterfly House

Once you set your butterfly house out in the garden, plant flowers that are known to attract butterflies. Just ask your garden retailer for suggestions. Milkweed is what caterpillars eat, so plant some near the house. A fairly long piece of bark should also be placed inside the house for the cocoon.

Examine the patterns, look at the photos, and read through the tips on page 111 before beginning the project.

TOOLS

Screwdriver

Saw

Workbench

Coping Saw

Pencil

Tape Measure

Clamp

Square

Plans: How the Butterfly House Goes Together

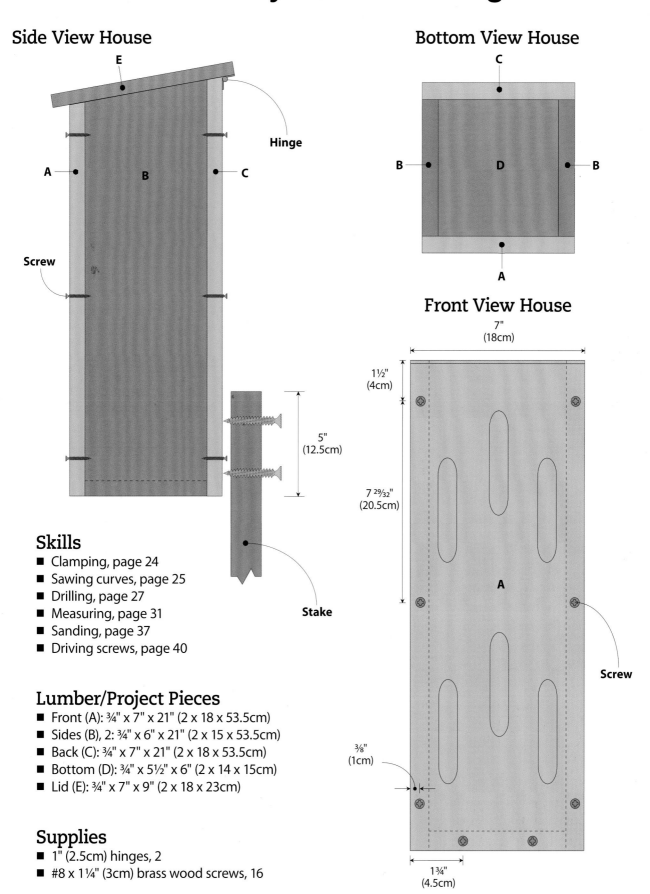

Side View House

E

A — B — C

Hinge

Screw

5"
(12.5cm)

Stake

Bottom View House

C

B — D — B

A

Front View House

7"
(18cm)

1½"
(4cm)

7 ²⁹⁄₃₂"
(20.5cm)

A

Screw

⅜"
(1cm)

1¾"
(4.5cm)

Skills

- Clamping, page 24
- Sawing curves, page 25
- Drilling, page 27
- Measuring, page 31
- Sanding, page 37
- Driving screws, page 40

Lumber/Project Pieces

- Front (A): ¾" x 7" x 21" (2 x 18 x 53.5cm)
- Sides (B), 2: ¾" x 6" x 21" (2 x 15 x 53.5cm)
- Back (C): ¾" x 7" x 21" (2 x 18 x 53.5cm)
- Bottom (D): ¾" x 5½" x 6" (2 x 14 x 15cm)
- Lid (E): ¾" x 7" x 9" (2 x 18 x 23cm)

Supplies

- 1" (2.5cm) hinges, 2
- #8 x 1¼" (3cm) brass wood screws, 16

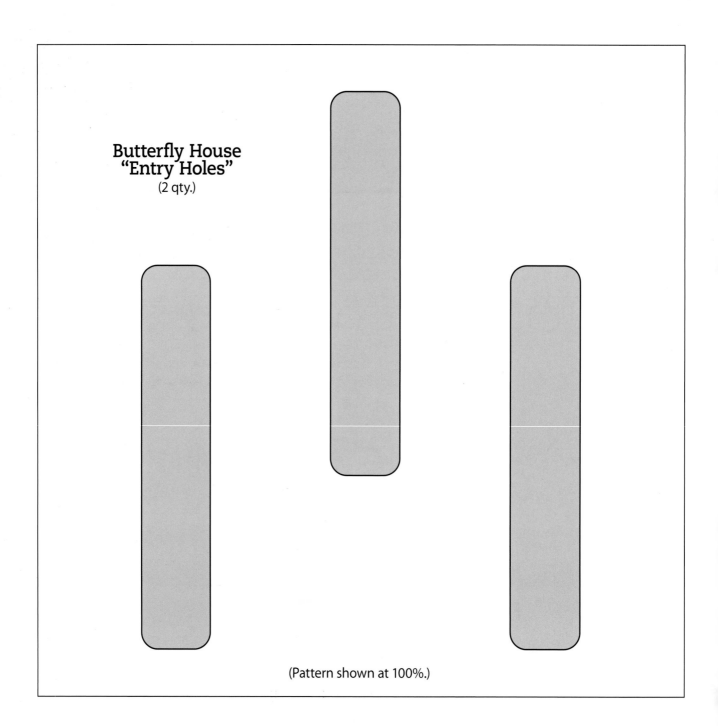

**Butterfly House
"Entry Holes"**
(2 qty.)

(Pattern shown at 100%.)

Building: **Butterfly House**

Here are some tips for building your butterfly house.

Counter Boring. The front and back blanks are fastened to the sides and bottom blanks with the brass screws. Refer to the front view house drawing for screw locations.

Partial Assembly. Cut the bottom to the dimensions given. Orient each piece by first laying a side blank down on the worktable. Place the bottom onto the side blank and flush with the side bottom edge; align the front and back blanks flush with the bottom. Screw the brass screws into the sides and bottom.

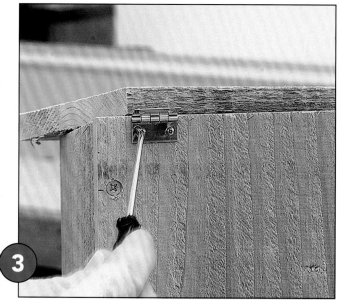

Hinges. Hinges are used on the lid to help in placing the proper feed inside the butterfly house. Cut the lid to the dimensions given. Each hinge is attached to the back and the lid. Measure in 1" (2.5cm) from the back edge for hinge placement. Center the lid on the house and mark for hinge placement.

Stake Attachment. Attach a stake to the bottom of the house with wood screws or nails. Measure up 5" (12.5cm) from the bottom of the house. Center the stake on the back of the house and fasten it.

More Great Books from Fox Chapel Publishing

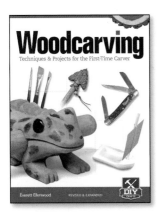

**Woodcarving,
Revised and Expanded**
ISBN 978-1-56523-800-8 **$14.99**

**Woodworker's & DIY
Pocket Guide, 2nd Edition**
ISBN 978-1-56523-811-4 **$9.99**

**Great Book of Shop
Drawings for Craftsman
Furniture, Revised Edition**
ISBN 978-1-56523-812-1 **$29.99**

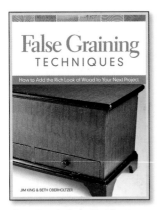

False Graining Techniques
ISBN 978-1-56523-797-1 **$11.99**

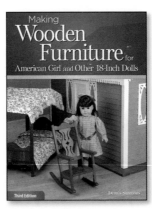

**Making Wooden Furniture
for American Girl® and Other
18-Inch Dolls, 3rd Edition**
ISBN 978-1-56523-793-3 **$19.99**

Wood Pallet Projects
ISBN 978-1-56523-544-1 **$19.99**

**How to Make Outdoor
& Garden Furniture**
ISBN 978-1-56523-765-0 **$22.99**

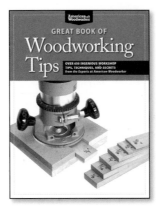

**Great Book of
Woodworking Tips**
ISBN 978-1-56523-596-0 **$24.95**

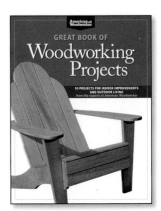

**Great Book of
Woodworking Projects**
ISBN 978-1-56523-504-5 **$24.95**